A Head Full
of Everything

A Head Full of Everything

Inspiration for Teenagers with the World on Their Mind

Gavin Oattes

CAPSTONE
A Wiley Brand

Registered office

John Wiley & Sons Ltd, The Atrium, Southern Gate, Chichester, West Sussex, PO19 8SQ, United Kingdom

Editorial Office
John Wiley & Sons Ltd, The Atrium, Southern Gate, Chichester, West Sussex, PO19 8SQ, United Kingdom

For details of our global editorial offices, customer services, and more information about Wiley products visit us at www.wiley.com.

Wiley also publishes its books in a variety of electronic formats and by print-on-demand. Some content that appears in standard print versions of this book may not be available in other formats.

Designations used by companies to distinguish their products are often claimed as trademarks. All brand names and product names used in this book are trade names, service marks, trademarks or registered trademarks of their respective owners. The publisher is not associated with any product or vendor mentioned in this book.

Library of Congress Cataloging-in-Publication Data

Names: Oattes, Gavin, 1979- author. | John Wiley & Sons, publisher.
Title: A head full of everything : inspiration for teenagers with the world on their mind / Gavin Oattes.
Description: Hoboken, NJ : Wiley, 2022. | Includes index.
Identifiers: LCCN 2021052114 (print) | LCCN 2021052115 (ebook) | ISBN 9780857089014 (paperback) | ISBN 9780857089052 (adobe pdf) | ISBN 9780857089021 (epub)
Subjects: LCSH: Teenagers—Life skills guides. | Self-esteem in adolescence. | Teenagers—Conduct of life.
Classification: LCC BF724.3.S36 O26 2022 (print) | LCC BF724.3.S36 (ebook) | DDC 155.5/182—dc23/eng/20211108
LC record available at https://lccn.loc.gov/2021052114
LC ebook record available at https://lccn.loc.gov/2021052115

Cover & Interior illustrations: Peter Cotter

Printed in Great Britain by Bell and Bain Ltd, Glasgow

For the ones who worry, the ones who dream,
and the ones forever being told to sort and
put away the washing.

Contents

The Bit Before The Beginning

Now, before we get properly started here, I'm keen to get something out of the way.

I know there's likely to be only one real reason for you to be reading this book, and that is your parents bought you it, right? Possibly even a teacher, but my money is on the parents!

Why? Because 'It might be helpful'. There is of course a chance you bought it for yourself which is totally cool but I'm guessing for most, this book was gifted to you.

It just means that if you *were* given it by your parents then you've probably questioned the real reason for them giving you it, i.e. exactly what is it they think I need help with?!

And based entirely on the fact it's a gift from your parents, I'm probably going to have to work a bit harder to prove to you this book is actually a proper kick-ass read. And even now you've just questioned the fact I used the phrase 'kick-ass'. Damn those parents!

But whatever the basis is for you now owning a copy, you've got it in your hands for a reason. Something out there brought you to this point and you're currently at the 'opening few pages stage' of this book, in other words over the next few pages you'll be trying to decide if you'll keep reading or not? And, well, you've probably questioned just who the author is, what age he is and what does he know about being a teenager!

Please allow me to introduce myself, I promise to keep it brief. . . .

My name is Gavin Oattes, I stand on stage, and words come out of my face.

Ok, maybe that's too brief!

I basically get booked to write and deliver talks for awesome companies such as Nike. Even cooler though is the fact I sometimes get to speak to extraordinary organisations such as the NHS. But the coolest part of my job is speaking to teenagers.

I started out in comedy as a teenager. In the beginning people told me to get a proper job. I tried that but really missed the 'not so proper job'. So I took the proper job, and the not so proper job, stuck them together and somehow ended up running a business that I love. And having now worked with over 1.5 million teenagers and some of the biggest companies in the world, someone has had the crazy idea to let me write books! I'm just going to go with it and who knows, maybe this way I'll get to make a bigger difference and work with millions more.

You see that's my goal, to make a difference in the world. That's it. I had no plans to be an entrepreneur, I'm not academic, I worry loads, I'm not cool, I can't sit still, I've failed hundreds of times, I overthink things and I doubt myself every day. But I work really hard and I love what I do.

Oh, and I love to swear. Please note, I only use the occasional mild sweary word in this book or else I'd get into trouble. In fact, I'll probably still get into trouble. You'll notice though, whilst I might occasionally say bad words, I *don't* say bad things . . . there is a difference!

So back to whether you'll keep reading or not. That's technically my job, so let me tell you this; this book might just change your life. At the very least it will challenge your thinking and give you a good laugh along the way. And I promise, it *will* help you.

'Help me with what?' I hear you ask. You see, we all need help from time to time but that's a question only you can answer.

I just need you to do two things . . . keep an open mind and pop your phone on silent!

'You'll turn out ordinary if you're not careful.'

—*Ann Brashares*

CHAPTER 1

Somewhere Now

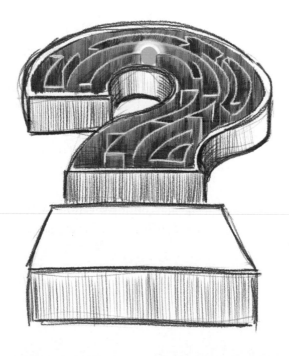

Being a teenager is brilliant and shite.

Now, there's a sentence that's never been written at the start of any book ever. Until now, obviously. A famous author once told me, 'Be sure to always start with a bold statement, Gavin!'

So, there's my bold statement. To be honest I could probably finish the book there too. A one sentence book. A one pager that would make more sense to teenagers than any other book ever written.

 Being a teenager is brilliant and shite. The end.

Technically that's two sentences, but you get the idea!

Life gives us 7 years of teenagering. In the grand scheme of things, it's not a lot. And yet, it's EVERYTHING when you're in it. 7 years, that's 84 months of change, 364 weeks of weird and 2,555 days of WTAF!

Life throws everything it can at us during this time. All the highs, all the lows and *everything* in between. It's the ultimate sandwich of life. Kid life on one side, grown-up life on the other. And in the middle, 61,320 hours of scrolling and inconvenience.

3,681,644 minutes. Every single one a gift.

Yes, a gift.

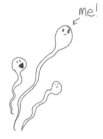

After all, you're lucky to be here. Of all the 100 million sperm, it was you. That, dear reader, is a very big thought and one that probably makes you want to throw up in your own mouth. But, it's also true. We are all lucky to be here. And the fact we get to 'teenager' for a while is really pretty special.

Parents tell us our teenage years are 'the best years of our life'. They can be, but the truth is, most grown-ups have forgotten that, sometimes, our teenage years are also horrendous.

Teenagers are completely misunderstood. The reality is, being a teenager is just like being a toddler all over again. Toddlers are always trying to discover their world in new and exciting ways, because they don't know anything about it.

You're also trying to discover the world too. But this time you've got every single stress imaginable on your shoulders. Friends, looks, parents, social media, exams, boys, girls, expectations, etc., etc.

The media paints a picture. They tell us you're all obsessed with sex and drugs. Apparently, you all sit on a lot of benches and get drunk, causing trouble.

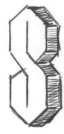 Anytime I was unhappy or going through a tough time, my parents used to tell me it was down to hormones. Great, thanks for the helpful advice during this awful experience that I'm having, glad to hear it's just hormones. . . .

Truth is, teenagers are decent human beings. I'm pretty sure you know very well that the choices you make now will affect the rest of your life. You don't need to hear this every single day. There's not a single teenager out there who aspires to live a life of regret.

For many it sucks to be a teenager. Treated like a child, expected to act like an adult.

Well, I've written this book to show you it doesn't have to suck. And when it does, there's some cool things you can do to make it suck a little less. See, you're not a child and you're not quite a proper adult yet either. You're a teenager.

When I was 11, I thought life would be better when I was a teenager. At 13, I couldn't wait to be 15. At 15, I was chasing 17. And at 17, I just wanted to be 21.

It all moves so fast and many of us are in such a hurry to grow up that we forget what it means to be young. Many are so focussed on the future that they forget to enjoy where they're at, right now.

What's the rush? Slow down.

In fact, let's slow down so much for a moment and put things firmly in reverse. . . .

Thiiiiiiiiiis Much Excited!

Think back to when you were 5 years old. Everything was magic. Even school, right from day 1.

I was reminded of this when my own son started school.

'YOU'VE GOT A SON, GAV?! JUST HOW OLD ARE YOU?' We'll get to this later. . . .

My son's name is Kian and at only 5 years of age he served up a perfect – and very much needed – lesson in life. And I'll never forget it.

His first day at school was, bizarrely, a Friday. It was a two-hour taster visit and then he'd start his first full day the following week. I woke up on the Monday of that week to discover Kian stood beside me at 6 am dressed in full school uniform. I reminded him that his first day was in fact Friday.

'I know,' he replied firmly, 'can't you tell what I'm doing?'

I thought about it and replied, 'No idea!'

'I'm practising.'

He practised on Tuesday, he practised on Wednesday and of course on Thursday. He forgot on the actual Friday, but we'll let him off as he was knackered from all his early mornings, but that's not the point.

I woke him on Friday, and he leaped out of bed, threw his uniform on and came sprinting into our room. My wife and I smiled weary early-morning-parenting smiles.

I told Kian that I'd never seen him this excited before in his entire life. He agreed wholeheartedly.

'That's because I've never been this excited in my entire life.'

There was a brief pause before he delivered the best bit.

'And I've been alive for five years!'

'In fact Dad, I'll show you how excited I am. I am THIIIIIS MUCH EXCITED!'

Please picture a 5-year-old with his arms stretched so wide they're almost touching behind his back. Shoulder blades touching.

As a teenager, you can probably remember being 5. Pretty much everything's exciting at that age, so to be beyond 'normal' excitement and to have ventured into 'THIIIIIS much excited' – we're in 'Christmas Eve/Disneyland' territory. Or 'Disneyland on Christmas Eve' territory, something of which I have never experienced but I can begin to imagine just how exciting this is.

That morning, my wife and I had a wonderful discussion about how, in that moment, there were thousands of young kids all waking up feeling the same – buzzing, pumped and ready to go. Raring to throw themselves into the next step of life's adventure. The same adventure that you're still on.

We continued to talk about how amazing it is that some people remain like that throughout life. Every single step of the journey, we meet them, the infectious energy they have, the buzz.

And then we had a really weird discussion about how some people never feel like that again. Something goes, fizzles out, vanishing entirely for some.

Could it be that some people peak at 5?

There is, of course, a downside to taking the next step in your adventure. Fear. Worry. Stress. Anxiety. You are excited and yet it's tinged with what might go wrong. It might not work. Failure is an actual thing. You know because, as a teenager, you've experienced it.

But when you're 4 or 5 these feelings can be somewhat new and confusing.

Fee-Fi-Fo-Fum

So there I was, week 1 of Primary School. Five years old and learning to fit in, whatever that means.

It was Friday, the final day of week 1. My school experience so far had been outstanding. New friends, old friends, Hide 'n' Seek and as much 'Heads Down Thumbs Up' as I could possibly imagine.

Magic.

We came back into the class after Playtime fresh from a game of 'Tig'. The Head Teacher, Miss Smart (real name) popped in for a chat.

'Good Morning boys and girls.'

'Goooooood Mmmmoooorrnning Miiiisss Smaart.'

Miss Smart was about to tell us something that would be a game changer for me.

'Boys and girls, for the first time ever, this Christmas, we are going to put on a school pantomime.'

I couldn't believe what I was hearing. A pantomime, in my new school. I loved pantomime.

'Not only are we putting on a pantomime boys and girls but we need some of *you* to be in it.'

Well, this just about sent me over the edge. My school were putting on a pantomime and some of *us* were going to be in it! I couldn't wait to tell my mum and dad.

'The Pantomime we will be doing this year is Jack & The Beanstalk.'

My absolute favourite pantomime ever. I could see it in my mind. The giant's enormous mechanical legs walking across the stage as 'fee-fi-fo-fum' rings out across the theatre.

'We need 5 pupils from this class to be the mice who run on stage every night and steal the giant's cheese.'

Mind. Blown.

 I was imagining myself sitting in the audience with snacks-a-plenty. I could see the mice, the cheese and again, the giant's legs. And me. I could picture it. It was going to be hilarious.

I was experiencing an excitement I had never felt before. A rush of pure adrenaline that felt magic. It was new to me, and I liked it. I liked it a lot.

Throughout life we are presented with opportunities. I was about to be presented with one that would ultimately shape my entire life. I kid you not, what happens next changed everything for me.

Remember, I was 5.

'Hands up if you want to be one of the mice in the pantomime?'

My hand was up the second she even began to say the word 'hands'. Imagine the fastest hand in the world. My hand was faster than this. Look at your own hand right now (I dare you). Go on, look at it and move it up in to the air as fast as you can. So, the speed at which you just moved is amateur compared to the speed I moved my entire arm this day as a five year old. Try again . . . still too slow. I was an actual ninja.

'Gavin Oattes.'

She picked me! This was it; this was my moment.

'Your hand was up first; do you want to be a mouse?'

All of a sudden I could picture the audience from the stage. It was like the camera in my head spun around 180 degrees. Now there were hundreds of people sitting watching me.

What if it went wrong? What if they didn't enjoy it? What if I wasn't good enough? What if no one turned up?

'Everything you want is on the other side of fear.'

—*Jack Canfield*

Where were all these questions coming from?

My wonderful feeling of unbelievable excitement turned to a much lesser wonderful feeling of unbelievable fear. I was scared, but this was not a scared I had ever felt before. This was new and I didn't like it.

My heart started to pound. I could hear the blood passing through my ears, my chest felt like it was crunching gears and my heart was racing faster than ever before. Shaking, nausea, numbness and of course impending doom.

I was 5. I just wanted to be a mouse, I really did. More than anything in the world, but something, something deep inside was stopping me.

It felt like I was going to be sick. My stomach hurt. This was a horrendous feeling of what I now know to be anxiety and what I came to discover as 'caring way too much about what people think of me.'

Now at this moment it's important for me to be clear on something. . . .

There are moments in life you should absolutely care. You really should, but only about things that set your soul on fire. As a human you need to save your energy for magical moments.

'Do you want to be a mouse?' Miss Smart repeated.

Again, all I could see was the audience staring back at me. All of a sudden I knew what it meant to be a worrier.

'No thanks, I only put my hand up because I need to go to the toilet.'

Everyone laughed. I can distinctly remember thinking 'Something's wrong, something's wrong, something's wrong' over and over again.

My teacher stepped in. . . .

'Are you sure Gavin, you seemed awfully excited.'

I had to get out. I repeated myself.

'I only put my hand up because I need to go to the toilet.'

'Ok then, on you go,' she said as I ran out the door.

I ran all the way to the toilet, ran into a cubicle, locked the door and burst into tears. I had never felt like this before. Five years old and I felt like my world had come to an end.

Why was I feeling like this over a pantomime?

Might seem a little over dramatic but to put this into a 5 year old's perspective, it was my absolute dream to be in a pantomime. I had always wanted to be in one. This was my magical moment. I had my chance and I blew it.

Because I was scared.

Seven years of primary school passed and not once did I set foot on a stage. Not once did I volunteer for anything that involved possible public humiliation.

That moment has stuck with me forever. I allowed the fear to get the better of me. That day affected my confidence for a very long time. It still does.

Then came high school. By this point I knew one day I'd be on the stage. Even with all the fears and all my anxieties, I just knew.

But, I continued to turn down every chance I had to get up and perform, I was so worried about what others might think. I didn't pick drama and no matter how much I wanted to, I didn't audition for school shows. More opportunities passed. Even reading aloud from a book in class became an issue for me. My face would turn bright red and my classmates would laugh.

'Oattesie's taking a beamer,' they would say. You'll know how much this can knock a teenager's confidence, even if done in jest.

Every day I dreamed of being on stage, performing and entertaining for hundreds (maybe thousands one day) of people in a theatre. It was the first thing I thought of in the morning and the last thing at night.

By 15 years of age, I was obsessed with comedy. Stand-up comedy, comedy films, TV shows, books, basically anything that was really silly and made me laugh. I would sit in my room at night writing comedy sketches, filling notebook after notebook with all the nonsense stored in my brain.

Maybe one day I would get to share this nonsense with the world.

Just one problem. I was still terrified by the thought of being on stage.

Navel-Gazing

I reckon people are a bit like belly buttons. Some of us are introverts (innies), some of us are extroverts (outies) and some are somewhere in the middle (inbetweenies).

It doesn't matter who you are, where you're from or what anyone else thinks of you. You are allowed to believe in you. You are allowed to be confident in you. You are allowed to step out of your comfort zone and when you spot an opportunity that looks and feels right, grab on with two hands, keep your feet on the ground and run as fast as you can.

If you don't then one day you might just look back and wonder, what if?

Just one thing. You are also allowed to be scared. It's normal.

So to the Innies, Outies and Inbetweenies, all of you, you're all wonderful. And beautiful. And weird. And magical.

Yeah, all of you.

Life goes by in a blur. We need to stop the navel-gazing and go make things happen.

I can remember teachers at school telling me to get my head out of the clouds. I think children should be encouraged to get their heads *back* in the clouds. *Teenagers* need to get their heads back in the clouds too, I need to get my head back in the clouds and the chances are *you* need to get your head back in the clouds. And start dreaming again. Like, proper dreaming, not sleep dreams. Actual proper big dreams that excite you and get your heart racing. The kind of thing that gets you out of bed with an extra spring in your step.

The problem most of us have in achieving our dreams is our thinking. Our thinking helps us to quit, to not try. We've all felt it.

But it's our thinking, and only our thinking, that will help us to succeed.

Dear Parents,

Remember when you started to want your own independence?

Guess where I'm at in life?

Kind regards,

Your Teenager

X

So, what about you? Did you wake up this morning feeling THIIIIIS much excited?

How often do you wake up on a Monday morning pumped, buzzing and raring to go? Are you waking up every single day energized, happy, driven and oozing passion?

I'm not talking about some days or most days, I mean EVERY SINGLE DAY! If your answer is 'No' then there's a word for people like you: normal. It's absolutely normal. It's normal to not wake up every day genuinely pumped full of energy, buzzing, raring to go. When you go to school it's normal too. And when you start working, it's normal there as well. It's normal for a school to NOT have all their young people waking up every morning fit to burst with excitement at the prospect of Pythagoras' Theorem. If you skip into school 'oozing with passion', someone's going to be making you a doctor's appointment.

Think about this for a moment. It's normal. You're normal. It is now the norm to NOT have people waking up energized, buzzing and raring to go to school or work. To go do the things they have chosen to do, every single day. I'm going to say it once more. It's normal. And it doesn't sit well with me.

Question: Do you want 'normal'?

I'm willing to put money on it that every single one of you reading this book absolutely categorically do NOT want normal. I'm willing to wager that you are in fact looking for, working for, hoping for, striving for, dreaming about something absolutely extraordinary. Something exciting, engaging, purposeful, colourful – even a little bit scary? Something that makes a difference. Something that makes you feel THIIIIIS much excited. And *that* dear reader, makes you not normal.

Question: Are you putting in the effort to achieve it?

Can you imagine what would happen if you woke up every single day with the same fire in your belly for the day ahead that you had when you were 4? It would be extraordinary. Abnormal even. But can you imagine what you'd achieve? And how you'd feel? And the impact you'd have on the normal? It's a mix of frightening and enlightening, but in the most beautiful way you could ever imagine. Moreover, it's a mindset. A choice. And it costs nothing.

" I tried to be
normal once.
Worst two minutes
of my life. "

—*Anon*

Ready Salted

Let me share with you my favourite quote of all time. We all love a good motivational quote. Everyone does. It's incredible how powerful a few positive words can be. There's a lot of quotes in this book, all quite different from the norm, but you've probably started to work out that neither this book or I for that matter are particularly normal.

And for the record, I'm very comfortable with not being normal. I wasn't for a very long time. I reckon my '2,555 days of WTAF' consisted mainly of desperately trying to fit in and yet somewhat confusingly trying to determine how to stand out.

My conclusion?

Normal is boring.

Anyway, back to my quote!

This quote is by none other than Macauley Culkin. I'm pretty sure you'll know who Macauley is; if you don't, he was the wee boy in the *Home Alone* movies. Well, he was in the first two. I'm not sure if you even know that there are other *Home Alone* movies? Probably best to just stick with the first two. . . .

So yeah, we're starting a book for teenagers with Kevin. Kevin McAllister to be exact. The cute, cheeky and street-savvy 8-year-old that lit up our lives with booby-traps, mischief and a lovely cheese pizza just for him. Apparently – according to his cousin – 'he's what the French call les incompetents'.

Now, whether you are a fan of the Home Alone franchise or not, it's fair to say Kevin was anything but incompetent. He took us all on a journey, an exciting adventure that ultimately reminded us of the importance of love, bravery, family and making the most of what we have. Oh, and not relying on technology, particularly to wake us up before a flight!

The quote goes as follows:

'I've yet to find a level of enthusiasm that tops

"Holy shit look at this giant potato chip!"'

—*Macaulay Culkin*

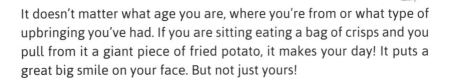

I love it.

Why?

Because it's true.

It doesn't matter what age you are, where you're from or what type of upbringing you've had. If you are sitting eating a bag of crisps and you pull from it a giant piece of fried potato, it makes your day! It puts a great big smile on your face. But not just yours!

Because, in that moment you turn to everyone else in the room and show it off. And you put a great big smile on their faces too. I'm not sure if you've ever realised this, but whenever you find any massive item of food, you always use your face as a comparative measuring tool.

'LOOK MUM, IT'S THE SIZE OF MY FACE!'

And of course, if there's no one else in the room, what do we do? Yup, we reach for our phones, take a quick pic and its on Snapchat, Tik Tok, Twitter, WhatsApp, Facebook, Instagram and whatever else there is these days for the whole world to see.

I guess I love the idea of being able to reach into an entirely normal moment, an everyday situation, and pull from it something that puts a smile on your face, lifts you, excites you or makes you laugh. But so much so you need to share it with others.

And that's my challenge to you with this book. Treat it as your very own big metaphorical bag of crisps and reach in. Pull from it something. *Something* is always a good starting point. It might not be the something you expected, it might be something small, something new or it might just be something that sets your soul on fire. It might be something that makes you laugh, makes you cry, it might even make you angry. But whatever you pull from this book, make sure it's something worth sharing with the world.

I had no plans to mention Macaulay Culkin, but ultimately his quote above is what this book is all about. Seeing the beauty and wonder in everything. Even the ordinary, the every day. Even a giant potato chip. It's about simplicity and appreciating all that's around you. Allowing ourselves to be excited at life, what it throws us, everything. It's about grit, bravery and passion. It's about rediscovering that childlike wonder, living in the moment, getting through all sorts of challenges and yes, having fun, lots of it, always.

I mentioned earlier that nobody is normal. But *being* a teenager is. And yet there is *nothing* normal about our teenage years.

So, this book isn't normal, you're not normal, I'm not normal, but being a teenager is entirely normal.

Confused? Good, yet another trait of being a successful teenager!

"You're a ghost driving a meat covered skeleton made from stardust, what do you have to be scared of?"

—*Anon*

Blow Your Own Mind for a Change!

We're born, we live and then we die. Now only two of these are really guaranteed. If you're reading this now, then you've definitely been born, which in itself – as previously mentioned – is extraordinary.

And guess what? You're *definitely* going to die. Again, blunt. But true.

Being born is mind-blowing, but it's easy. Not for Mum obviously, she does all the work, you did absolutely nothing. Like dying, it just happens. Neither are particularly pleasant or enjoyable for anyone but for the individual on their way in or out, easy-peasy.

But do you believe in life after delivery?

I've already said it, life can be rubbish. It requires energy and effort. It can feel like a chore but the more skilled at it we become, the better at it we get and the happier we feel.

We all have different thoughts and opinions when it comes to living our best life and what that even means. That's what keeps the world exciting, we're all different. But really, who has actually nailed living? Has anyone truly perfected life?

Nope, of course not. But we can give a go! And when better to give life a damn good go than in your teens.

Think back to when you were a wee kid and you saw your teacher *outside* of school, perhaps in the supermarket or in a restaurant. Remember how it made you feel? It was always one of life's real 'WOW' moments. It was exciting, mind-blowing, weird and incredibly warming all at once. And it kinda made us feel on edge a little.

This is how being a teenager can feel, sometimes daily. Why? Because being a teenager *is* exciting, mind-blowing, weird and incredibly warming.

And guess what? It kinda makes us feel on edge a little. This isn't just felt by teenagers though, this is what truly being alive should *always* feel like.

You're not 4 or 5 anymore. No one is expecting you to wake up every day buzzing. Now, depending on where you are from, the word 'buzzing' has many different meanings, but you know what I mean.

I'm talking about pinging out of bed with excitement and enthusiasm every single day, raring to go!

In most other books about teenagers, it's here they would present to you a whole bunch of science and aim to educate you all about your brain, demonstrating the changes that happen, in turn leading to the fact you no longer jump out of bed every morning excited about going for a poo and eating cereal.

But I told you this book is like you, it's not normal. So, instead, some more questions. . . .

Are you happy most of the time?

I'm going with 'most of the time' as we simply cannot be happy *all* the time.

Is there a great big, enormous fire in your belly for life?

What's the point in even having a belly if there's no fire in it, right? Think back to you when you were about 4 years old. The fire was stoked daily. Everything was exciting.

Experts tell us life is all about being in the moment, making the most of now, not worrying about the future and living life in the present. But you get to wrap that present up however you want it. Sounds a bit cheesy but life is like wrapping a present. Sometimes it just folds beautifully without even trying. That moment the scissors glide as if by magic and the sticky tape tears beautifully.

Then there's the moments where the paper creases, the scissors tear the paper, you've got the whole roll of tape stuck to the present, it's not folding anything like it should be but you're so past caring you just accept it for what it is. Then to add insult to injury, you've not measured it out properly, so you need to cut another piece and patch it up. You've half-assed it and for now it will have to do.

At 18 years of age, still scared, I finally decided to wrap my present up the way I had always dreamt. If there was ever a job for someone terrified of crowds, public humiliation and other people's opinions it certainly wasn't the world of comedy. So, naturally, I booked myself a gig, put myself on a stage and became a stand-up comedian. . . .

I did my first gig. It felt incredible. Over the last 20 years I have performed all over the world. Good gigs, terrible gigs, great gigs. So many ups and downs. I've met the most wonderful people and the main thing I have learned is this.

If you're faced with an opportunity that's both terrifying and amazing, then you should totally go for it.

Welcome to life. Teenage life. The weirdest 7 years you'll ever have. Terrifying and amazing. My challenge to you is to wrap your 7 years up however the hell you want to. Stop pretending to be normal, embrace your inner weird, never grow up, be you and be sure that for your 7 years, you act your age. Literally.

'No matter what you do, in the beginning it's going to suck, because you suck. But you'll get better, and you'll suck less. And as you keep doing this, eventually you'll suck so little, you'll actually be good.'

—*Garrett J. White*

CHAPTER

2

Head. Cloud.
Heart. Sleeve.

fell off my scooter the other day. When I say scooter, I mean an actual scooter. Not a moped with an engine. Not an electric scooter, a literal scooter. A kid's one. Except it's mine.

I was feeling particularly confident for a non-scooter stunt specialist. I figured I could do a bit of a jump while going full speed. Not even a spectacular jump, literally a bit of a jump.

I'm not sure if I hit a stone or crack in the pavement but my scooter stopped immediately. I didn't. I went over the top at what felt like 70 miles per hour and hit the ground at what felt like 100 miles per hour. If there was ever a word to describe how I hit the ground, it's

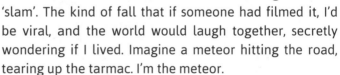

'slam'. The kind of fall that if someone had filmed it, I'd be viral, and the world would laugh together, secretly wondering if I lived. Imagine a meteor hitting the road, tearing up the tarmac. I'm the meteor.

I think overconfidence perhaps had something to do with it. I am now very, very sore. The thing is, sometimes our confidence can get us in trouble.

Did you know that 8% of males and 7% of females think they could beat a lion in a fist fight? This is definitely the kind of confidence that's going to get people in trouble.

We're told all through life from a very young age that confidence is key. The way one carries themselves, acts, stands, walks, talks and interacts with others. How you walk into the exam hall, that job interview or the first time you ask someone out, confidence matters. There even comes a day they tell us that confidence is an attractive trait for humans to have.

That explains why I was rubbish with exams *and* girls!

The thing is, there's believing in yourself and then there's downright delusion. Believing you can make a brilliant ham sandwich is confident, believing you can beat a lion in a fight is hilarious.

We all know someone who we could describe as overconfident. But is overconfidence really a thing, can we actually be *too* confident? Can confidence actually become a hindrance?

And, perhaps more importantly, what about those of us who lack confidence? Does it mean that unless we are bursting with confidence, we don't stand as good a chance as our peers at achieving greatness?

Are those of us who perhaps struggle with confidence also allowed to aim for greatness or does this now make us overly confident too?

Aaaaannd, do we even *need* to be aiming for greatness?

I'm confused.

Just as well the experts at the Institute for the Psychology of Elite Performance at Bangor University have extensively examined this very thing.

The reason I'm interested in this stuff is because I lack confidence. I'm more than comfortable sharing this with you. People don't tend to believe this because of my job. They see me on a stage doing what I do, they read my books and they assume my levels of confidence are intact. Truth is, I doubt myself regularly and beat myself up about it daily. I always have and it drives me crazy. So, I'm keen to know what the possible outcomes of this are.

Firstly, what is low confidence? I'm told low confidence is the state of thinking that we are not quite ready to face an upcoming task. Cool, check. That's me all the time, it was me all through school and it's me now, pacing up and down backstage, wondering why I'm doing this, questioning why anyone is going to listen to me!

So, what happens then when we are lacking in confidence? Well, in this case, one of two things happens: either we disengage from the task . . . not ideal. Or we invest extra effort into preparing for it.

Not all bad then.

In one of the studies, participants were required to skip with a rope continuously for one minute. Participants were then told that they had to repeat the task but using a more difficult rope to skip with (in fact it was the exact same type of rope). Results revealed that confidence actually decreased **but** performance improved.

Sooooo, what you're telling me is that self-doubt can be quite beneficial? Exactly. It can, in many ways, make us better. It can, in fact lead to an increase in effort, we try harder.

Now let's consider the role of overconfidence. A high level of confidence is usually helpful for performing tasks because it can lead you to strive for difficult goals. But high confidence can also be detrimental when it causes you to lower the amount of effort you give towards these goals.

Overconfidence often makes people no longer feel the need to invest all of their effort – think of that person you know who studies less for upcoming exams.

Interestingly, research shows that when you believe you are better than you really are, it will have a negative effect on whatever the task is at hand and your performance essentially dips.

Unfortunately, there is another common side effect to overconfidence, it's called dickheadedness. We all know one.

So, this is good news for those of us who lack confidence but still care enough to want to do well and give our all in life . . . and maybe even dare to be great at something?

Don't Let the World Make You Normal

Let's be honest, the world isn't going to change to accommodate you. If you're waiting for everything to fall into place, for that perfect moment, and only then will you start living your best life – you'll die waiting.

'Don't ask yourself what the world needs. Ask yourself what makes you come alive, and go do that, because what the world needs is people who have come alive.'

—Howard Thurman

The modern world is, on the whole, rather amazing. Yes, I know the news is bad, social media gets our back up and parents go on about everything being better back in the day. But I'm not convinced by that argument. I said the modern world was 'amazing', not 'perfect'. Modern life throws up all sorts of obstacles to our wellbeing. We're not built to sit in our bedrooms all day, staring at screens. We're not built to be alone. We're not built to fill our bodies with junk food and energy drinks. We're not built to stay still.

We're built to move, run, jump and even dance. We're built for the outdoors. We're built to learn, to be creative. We're built for communities, togetherness and to be part of a movement. We're built to eat wholesome foodstuffs and drink water. We're built to grow and get better.

What's really cool, is that right now, at your age, you can start to build the world you want for you. Unfortunately, for many years, humans haven't always got this right. We have in so many ways got it very, very wrong.

And the result is a tiredness. An unhealthiness. A mental ill-health.

But look closely at the world. The opposite is also true. There is an energy about it. A healthiness. A mental wellness. Sometimes we need to search hard to find it, but it's there. And you're allowed to be inspired by it, to learn from it, to absorb it, to contribute to it, to be a part of it, to lead it.

There's always time to chill. There's always time to scroll. There's always time to stop and do nothing, sometimes we need to! But it's too easy to do that *all* the time.

Sitting in your trackies, basking in the glow of your phone for hours on end won't get you to where you want to be. You've already worked out that the weeks are getting faster, time stops for no one.

Look, I'm pretty sure you're switched on to this stuff. You probably look after yourself more than the media would give you credit for.

But too many of us are tired. Bored. Fed up. Stressed. Angry.

I can assure you though, there is a solution and it's cheap.

No, it's not a Red Bull on the way to school. Or a Monster to get you through your studies. It's way more healthy than that. Your body and brain are not built for those drinks, hence the reason you would die if you drank too many of them. Literally, don't drink them, ever.

When I say the solution is cheap, it is. It doesn't cost any money, but it does cost time and energy. And better still, you're built to do it. . . .

What if the secret was in our heads – more specifically our thinking – and we could maintain some of that youthful, carefree exuberance that we had when we were 4, but now, in your teens *and* for the rest of your life before society snaps you up and pops you on the treadmill to Grownupsville?

It was a different kind of energy at that age, never forced. You weren't fussed about the news. Life excited you. You had zero issues with Mondays and puddles were not to be avoided.

'Only children believe they're capable of everything.'

—*Paulo Coelho*

Growing Up Is Optional

Think back to when you were about 7 years old and your teacher gave you a reading book that you had already read the year before with your previous teacher.

How'd that make you feel?

I'll tell you how it made the kids feel the first time I made that mistake as a teacher.

Furious. They were furious with me.

Why?

Because at the age of 7, we want nothing more than to be moved up a reading level. The only thing we want more than that is for all our classmates to see, hear and hopefully acknowledge that we've been moved up!

In fact, the only thing we want more than this is to see the look of pride on our parents' faces.

This was one of the many things that amazed me during my time as a teacher.

'HANG ON, YOU'RE A TEACHER, GAV? WHEN WERE YOU GOING TO TELL US THIS?!'

Ok, so I managed to squeeze in a teaching degree along the way. I'm qualified to teach kids aged 3–12.

Every single day as a primary school teacher young kids amazed me. There are so many moments of inspiration. Like when the queues form at the teacher's desk. You've all stood in those queues. There are loads of reasons why kids stand in them but there's 2 big ones.

The first is to ask for help. This really is a biggie.

I like to imagine we're all born with the unique ability to ask for help. It's such a natural thing to ask for when we're very young. But it's like we un-learn this skill. By the time we've hit our teens asking for help can feel silly, embarrassing or even weak. There is nothing weak in asking for help, in fact, quite the opposite. Asking for help is what makes us stronger. It connects us with others, allowing us to surround ourselves with people that make us feel good and encourage all sorts of new learning and adventure. Asking for help can create optimism and hope. Be sure to do it more.

Another thing that always amazed me as a primary school teacher was those moments I was sitting doing my work as all the kids were doing theirs, and the queue formed to my right-hand side. Now we've all stood in that queue, we know what it's like. It usually consists of a row of children with great big smiles on their faces, saying something along the lines of 'I'm finished, what's next?' It's like an absolute need at that age, a want and desire to learn, to progress, to prove themselves and to embrace the next challenge. We don't care what others think. We're ready, willing and more than able to take on the world, to be the best we can be, to dream and to think big.

You see, this is what inspires me most about wee kids. They always want to know what's next. They crave information and every single day as a teacher my mind was completely and utterly blown by the energy, passion, excitement and drive that those wee kids had, simply for what's next.

But there's a problem with being that age. And it's this . . .

We stop being that age.

That's it.

I'll say it again.

We stop being that age.

There's a technical term for it: 'growing up'.

We leave primary school . . . and off we go into Teenagerland. You may also call it high school. A magical land filled with hopes and dreams. A future-focussed paradise filled with ambition and desire. A training ground for growing up, fitting in and dealing with change.

Some people consider it a breeze; others do not. Some people consider it a portal to a better life; others do not. Some people consider it a prison full of assholes; others do not.

Everyone thinks differently when it comes to high school. One thing I *can* guarantee, however, is that in Teenagerland we do our most thinking. Not necessarily our *best* thinking but we definitely do our *most* thinking.

But it is our thinking and thinking alone that will determine the experience we have as a teenager. And as all the experts tell us, happiness doesn't come from things, it comes from experiences.

Dear Parents,

Guess what? My brain is kind
of broken just now.
I literally don't think like you.
It's called science, Google it.

Your Teenager

x

Broccoli and Eyeballs

I believe that in growing up too many of us lose something special. Very special. Some hold on to it forever, for others it comes and goes, but for many, it just disappears entirely. I'm going to refer to it as 'that wee piece of magic'. It's a natural thing that we're all born with. I see it in my own two kids every day.

So what do I actually mean by 'that wee piece of magic'? Let me try and explain. . . . About three months before my son's 5th birthday we woke at 4 am to the sound of him screaming 'DAAAAD' as loud as he possibly could. I got the fright of my life and leapt out my bed.

In fact, I didn't even touch the bed, I just landed on two feet and ran for the door (because that's how ninjas respond). As I headed for the door Kian came running into the room still shouting, 'DAAAAD!' Obviously concerned, I stopped him and asked 'What on earth is it Kian? It's 4 in the morning. What's the matter?'

Perfectly calm, Kian smiled and simply answered, 'I know why they're called eyeballs.' This for me was a moment of magic. Let me explain why.

The fact that it was 4 am is irrelevant when the star of the story is only 4. Kian had woken up and had a moment of learning, which is cool but it's not the moment of magic. The moment of magic came next. He shared it. That's it. It's that simple. He shared it. Because that's what you do when you're 4, you share stuff. Doesn't matter what you experience or what you discover, you share it. Doesn't matter how big it is or how small it is, you share it. Doesn't matter how exciting it is or how boring it is, how colourful or dull, you share it, because you're 4.

But at nearly 5, you don't just share it. You share it from here (*points to chest*), with heart and soul. With passion, energy, excitement and it's always wrapped up in a big ball of wonder. It's beautiful. It's magic.

So why is this relevant to you – a teenager – reading this? How many times in your life have you been asked at school to share your work, share your knowledge, your inspirations, your ideas, to share who you are? And how often do you actually share, from here (*points to chest*), with heart and soul? With passion, energy and excitement all wrapped up in a big ball of wonder?

There's how the best leaders lead. There's how we create a movement. There's how we inspire. There's how we make a difference. There's how we change the world.

And in case you're wondering, Kian never actually told me why they're called eyeballs. To be fair, that wasn't the point.

I'll give you one more example of this wee piece of magic I speak of.

We were having dinner one night. There was broccoli on the plate. Now I don't like broccoli, but my kids love it. They're weird, right? I had broccoli on my plate because that's a good parenting example. My son leant over, picked up a piece of broccoli from my plate and said, 'Dad, you should eat your greens,' to which I replied, 'And you should stop touching my food.' 'Broccoli is great fun dad.' I had never heard this sentence before.

He continued, 'it can beee stuff'. Now, instantly my brain showed me lots of pictures of trees. We all know broccoli looks like trees, yours probably just did the same. It turned out I was on the right lines, but as he was only 4, he was streets ahead of me. Holding up the piece of broccoli he said, 'See this piece here Dad, I want you to imagine it's summertime, in fact no Dad' – he bit the head off the broccoli – 'it's autumn.'

Genius. I sat there thinking isn't it incredible how at such a young age we can take anything we want and transform it into anything we want? Anything.

Of course, at such a young age we find this process much more natural. Firstly, as kids we always want things to be better, to be more fun, more exciting. Secondly, we believe it to be possible. And lastly, we know it will be worth the effort.

What do I mean by that last one?

It's why young kids will sit and build Lego for 4 hours then knock it down and start again. It's why they'll go outside and build a den even though they've been told it's going to rain in an hour.

This example right here, with the den and the rain. This sums up for me just what goes wrong for so many of us out there. There are simply too many people – teens included – who have made a shift from being the type of person who thinks and says 'I'm going outside to build a den in the garden' to being the type of person that thinks and says 'but it's going to rain in an hour'.

'Once you're grown up, you can't come back.'

—*Peter Pan*

That's the wee piece of magic I'm talking about right there. Heading outside to build the den or staying indoors to wait for the rain to pass. It's the perfect metaphor for life.

It's the difference between actually *building* the den and *wishing* you'd built the den. The difference between doing something that excites you and doing something safer. The difference between embracing the moment or passing it up. The difference between getting stuck in no matter what and sitting this one out.

Think about this from your perspective as a teenager. Like really young kids, most teenagers want things to be better, to always be improving. Most will seek some kind of positive change. We all want to have fun. Step one is always the easy part.

Step two is where we lose some people. It becomes harder to believe some things are possible. As we enter adulthood, we now know what it's like to fail, to be judged, to be told we're not good enough. We worry more about other people's opinions. We start to overthink things. We can overthink things to such an extent we convince ourselves we can't do or have certain things, so it's easier to not even try.

And then there's step three, as teenagers we know what it means to be told 'the effort will be worth it in the long run'. It's code for 'in the short-term it's going to be awful'. Like exams. 'Put the effort in now and it will all pay off' they say. What they're really saying is that it's going to be stressful, messy and we're all going to be exhausted.

When you're in proper groan-up jobland, they'll say things to you like, 'we're embarking on a journey of change' or 'we're going on a journey of growth'.

We are *ALWAYS* on a journey of growth! BUT PLEASE CAN WE STOP CALLING IT 'A JOURNEY OF GROWTH'!!! It's just life.

It won't matter what age you are, or how boring your boss is, it will be the wee piece of magic that gets you through. But not just through . . . in, involved and engaged.

But how do we do this? How do we make sure we never lose that wee piece of magic?

Mindset.

This is once again all about how you choose to think. I am a firm believer in the idea that *you are what you think*.

Change your thinking, you change your thoughts. Change your thoughts, you change the words that come out your mouth. Change the words that come out your mouth, you change what you give off.

Your thoughts lead to behaviours. Always.

I once read a beautiful quote by Cynthia Occelli: **'For a seed to achieve its greatest expression, it must come completely undone. The shell cracks, its insides come out and everything changes. To someone who doesn't understand growth, it would look like complete destruction.'**

Sound familiar? Welcome to the teenage years. Welcome to life.

At 4 years of age we don't see destruction. We see adventure and excitement, we just think 'bring it on'. As young adults, many of us see hard work, frustration and effort.

What if there's too much emphasis these days on striving to be great at something. This brings nothing but pressure and comparison. What if we've got it all wrong. Rather than finding the confidence to be great, what if it was about finding the confidence to have fun? To see the fun in the everyday, the fun in the ordinary. To play.

You used to be the best at playing. So did your parents. And your grandparents. I hope you've not forgotten this.

Remember when you were 6? In your mind you were never too far from a playground. The floor was always lava. Sometimes you played in the clouds. All steps were rainbow coloured. Every bridge was a shake shake bridge. You never sat still. Homework was fun. Museums came to life. The library was loud and you could borrow more than just books! Waiting never felt like waiting. Rain falling during school break time didn't mean we're staying indoors, it meant 'Get your wellies on!' It was like every day was national play day.

That wee boy/girl is still inside you. Still bursting with curiosity, still bursting with excitement. Still bursting with magic. The goal is to never let them disappear.

At that age there was nothing actually very hard about being playful. Far too many young people now worry about looking silly or doing something 'uncool'. We live in a time where we can hide behind screens, heavily influenced by other people's opinions.

More weight is given to tests and grades than ever. We now spend more time than ever in settings where we are directed, protected, catered to, ranked and judged.

When you are playful, you let go of all that.

'I find it amusing that we're all pretending to be normal when we could be insanely interesting instead.'

—*Atlas*

Hide 'n' Seek

A couple of years ago I was invited to speak at a TEDx event. This one was particularly special as it was to be held at St Andrews University, one of the most prestigious universities in the world. I was buzzing, couldn't wait to do my thing.

The theme for the day was all around play and rediscovering your inner child. Perfect!

I wanted to try something completely different. I decided my talk would be all about why so many grown-ups don't play anymore, and I wanted to come up with something that would prove it. What could I do in a lecture theatre with 300 grown-ups?

There's no way I could play Hide 'n' Seek, that would be crazy, no one would ever do that. And plus, it could never work in that kind of space. There's nowhere to hide!

And then I began to think, well, that would be perfect because if they really wanted to play then they'd find a way. But in this context it would play into my hands as they won't play – because it's crazy – so my point will be proved there and then. As adults we don't play anymore, certainly not the way we used to!

So, Hide 'n' Seek it was.

" **You're only given a little spark of madness, you mustn't lose it.** "

—Robin Williams

To set the scene quickly, St Andrews University is, *well*, fancy. I was nervous, partly because it was TEDx event and partly because I know fine well, I don't belong there, our future king and queen went to this university. To be blunt, these aren't my people.

My imposter syndrome was kicking off in all sorts of ways. My self-talk went as follows . . .

'Shut up Gav, they've asked you to be here, get in, attempt to play hide-and-seek and get out.'

That was it, that's all I had for myself in that moment. I honestly don't believe anyone in the entire history of man has had this thought before giving a presentation at St Andrews University.

The room filled quickly. 300 people. I was up first. I had 18 minutes.

'Ladies and Gentlemen, please put your hands together and welcome our first speaker, Gavin Oattes.'

I have this habit of forgetting everything I'm going to say as I walk on to the stage and then just as I open my mouth it all comes back to me. This day was no different. I walked on with nothing, opened my mouth and everything I had planned began to pour out my mouth. All the while knowing I was building towards my big hide-and-seek moment.

'So, I'm going to shut my eyes and I'm going to count to 10. And you're going to hide.'

There was a ripple of nervousness. In me, yes, but more so the auditorium!

'The rules are you're not allowed to leave the room.'

I'm thinking they'll all just sit there looking at me with a weird expression and this allows me to naturally roll into my main point that as adults we just don't play anymore the way we used to, because we grew up.

'If you've never played hide-and-seek before then you've got exactly 10 seconds of me counting to Google it and get running.'

I closed my eyes.

'1 . . .'

I hadn't even got to 2 seconds and all I heard was 300 seats pinging up and 300 people hitting the floor, leaping other seats, screaming, shoving, and laughing their heads off.

Once again my inner voice kicked in . . .

'Shit Gav, they're really doing it. You've got 300 people in a room at the poshest university in the world, it's a TEDx event, it's being filmed and they're playing hide-and-seek. Like, actual hide-and-seek.'

I shat it.

What do I do?

Then I had a moment.

A moment of pure magic. And here it is . . .

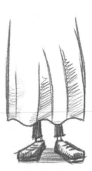

Give people the chance to play and they'll take it.

I'll repeat it.

Give people the chance to play and they'll take it.

Think about it. We love to play. You do, I do, we all do. And if you don't love to play then you've never played properly. You've being doing it wrong. Or you've forgotten. I reckon lots of people the world over have forgotten how to play and what it actually feels like to be in that moment.

But how often are you given the chance nowadays as a teenager? We're not wee kids anymore, *we* need *our* hand held. It's all back to front. You were once 4 and knew exactly what to do, right? But some teenagers have grown up and they've forgotten.

Forgotten how to play. Forgotten how to be in the moment. Forgotten how to see the fun in everything.

Maybe it's a confidence thing. Confidence to enjoy the journey, to create, build and grow . . . like the seed in the quote above.

But just like the seed we need water, space to move and grow, natural light, nourishment, looking after, help, encouragement.

And again, just like the seed, in time we become stronger, healthier, fresher, full of life, energy, magic and wonder.

But it's a marathon, not a sprint. Nothing will ruin your teens more than thinking you should have your life together already.

Let's repeat that. Nothing will ruin your teens more than thinking you should have your life together already.

And yes, I said magic and wonder.

" **Did you even have a childhood if you never sat round the kitchen table at a party with a Cadbury's chocolate bar frantically waiting to roll a 6 so you could throw on your hat, scarf and gloves and begin demolishing chocolate with a knife and fork?** "

—Anon

Don't Quit
the Daydream

Welcome to Paradise

'Dreams are lovely. But they are just dreams. Fleeting, ephemeral, pretty. But dreams do not come true just because you dream them. It's hard work that makes things happen. It's hard work that creates change.'

—*Shonda Rhimes*

Society isn't always truthful. In fact, it lies. A lot.

We have books, courses, TV adverts, multi-millionaires, TV personalities, YouTube sensations all selling us the same thing; the dream life.

The house, the car, the holidays, the career, the money, the clothes, the fame . . .

'You can be anything you want to be.'

'If you can dream it, you can do it.'

Sounds great, right? And easy, too. We are spoon-fed a conveyor belt of sexy slogans designed to inspire us into living our best lives.

The thing is, it just isn't true.

Of course you can't be anything you want to be! At 5 I wanted to be a rhinoceros, that's not going to happen, is it? And I regularly dream about being David Bowie, but hey, I'm not.

Ok, so I'm being a little facetious here, but my point stands. You simply cannot be *anything* you want to be. And just by dreaming of something doesn't mean you're guaranteed to achieve it.

And guess what? That's absolutely ok.

Perhaps if we took all the well-known slogans and re-worded them with something a lot less sexy but a bit more real, it might go like this . . .

You can't be anything you want to be, but if you have an idea, work hard, focus, stay curious, develop your skills, put yourself out there, take care of your mental health, don't be a dick, surround yourself with good people and then with a bit of luck/chance thrown in, then you can have a great time carving out a unique and interesting life for yourself. Oh, and it may or may not make you happy.

That's not going to sell books though, is it?

'Maybe the journey isn't so much about becoming anything. Maybe it's about un-becoming everything that isn't really you, so you can be who you were meant to be in the first place.'

—*Paul Coelho*

As I wrote earlier, the fun is in the journey, the creating, the finding out, the forming of new relationships, but so many get stuck, focussed on the end point, wondering just when the millions are going to roll into the bank, accompanied by a blue tick on social media.

I guess we all want *something* in life. But have you ever wanted something so bad it hurts? I can recall many occasions throughout my life having this feeling but then toying with the almost immediate follow-up thought of 'I'm not capable' or 'these things never happen to me'. So often I wanted the thing, but rarely did I ever think 'and I'm gonna make it'.

Except in comedy. I knew. I had always known. I had imagined it so hard that in my head it was a reality. Which made it extra difficult when it all came crashing down around me.

Of course, everything starts with an idea. Some might call it a dream. It's just what you then do with it. We're all dreamers. Again, this is ok. Some do it more than others. Some take it seriously, write it down, map it out, and others think it's childish. Some have decided there's no longer any point. It's silly, it's stupid, why bother?

When we're 5 years old we're actively encouraged to dream and think big and then by our teenage years we're told to grow up and stop daydreaming. Life becomes serious, it's time to become society. Pick a path and stick to it.

Society: Be yourself

Society: Not like that

There is one phrase that I remember from my teens. A teacher of mine had this on a poster on his classroom wall.

'You are only limited by your imagination'

You see, I believe this one . . .

Your brain is amazing.

Especially your imagination. But do you really know what it's capable of?

You might just think it allows you to think about stuff differently, but it's your imagination and your thoughts that create your future. Think about it, this is like a real-life superpower, you can see the future!

Throughout life you'll hear all sorts of people telling you that 'thoughts become things'. Albert Einstein said, 'Imagination is everything, it is the preview for life's coming attractions.'

It's all too easy to get stuck in life and feel like we're not moving forward but our imaginations allow us to focus on the real life that we want to experience. I'll come back to this point shortly.

Life sucks sometimes.

We all have moments in life that we wish had never happened. Death, sadness, sickness, fallouts with friends, that moment you step on dog shit, or worse, Lego. The list goes on.

Dear Parents,

Have you even made any effort to understand Pokémon? Maybe we'd talk more if you did.

Kind regards,

Your teenager x

But we also know life is magical at times.

Your imagination is what allows this to happen. It allows us to take the mundane and turn it into the magical. Again, it's your superpower. Think back to when you were 4 years old and someone handed you a cardboard box. What did you do with it?

Drove it. Flew it. Decorated it. Sailed it. Transformed it. Surfed it. Ate it.

You turned it into anything you wanted.

With your imagination.

I bet you are smiling as you are reading this. Taking a moment to remember what it was like to view the world through the eyes of a four-year-old reminds us of the joy and wonder the imagination brings.

So, I want to test your imagination right now.

On the opposite page I want you to write a letter to yourself from the four-year-old you, offering you some advice for life. Just what would the four-year-old you have to say? Go on, give it a bash. This exercise is done best sitting cross legged with crayons in one hand and Hula Hoops on your fingers. The carton of Ribena is optional, but I suggest sugar free. Just write the first thing that pops into your head. What would the four-year-old you be telling you to do with your life right now?

I bet it doesn't involve anything to do with social media, Wi-Fi or being a grown up. . . .

Dreamers Unite

So, let's get this right. . . .

We can't be 'anything you want to be' and dreams don't always come true, but with the help of our imagination we can bloody well try our best?

Correct.

It was my imagination that got me through my teens. My ability to imagine is really pretty awesome. It got me in trouble sometimes as I'm also very easily excited when it comes to new ideas. Some might call it 'distracted' rather than 'excited', call it what you want, I'm cool with both. If I'm distracted by something because it has caught my eye and lit a fire in my belly then what's the problem, right? I said I'd come back to this point. . . .

When times were hard, when life was heavy or exam pressure was building, I found that making time to map out what I wanted and where I was going in life brought some energy, some excitement. Remember, our imaginations allow us to focus on the real life that we want to experience. In other words, when things were a bit shit, with the help of my imagination I was able to see a way out, a more exciting road ahead. This allowed for a 'put in the effort now and it will all work out' kind of attitude. Remember this from earlier?

'If you don't design your own life plan, chances are you'll fall into someone else's plan. And guess what they have planned for you? Not much.'

—*Unknown*

There's just one problem; most of us give up on our dreams. And many give up early.

Don't worry, I'm not about to tell you to 'shoot for the stars', I don't want you to throw up on your lovely new book, but I am interested in the whole concept of dreaming big. There's a few different camps when it comes to this stuff.

Camp 1: Think huge, chuck everything at it, you're gonna smash it and live the dream!

Camp 2: Think huge, give it your best, you might make it, have a backup just in case!

Camp 3: Think realistically, have a robust plan, expect some failures, focus on a safe job, dip your toe in the water of dreams . . .

Camp 4: Get qualifications, get a secure job, have a fun hobby at the weekends.

Camp 5: Don't be ridiculous, it's just a stupid dream, you'll never make it, get a grip.

There's a select few of us in the world who don't think of it as silly or childish in any way to chase our dreams. We still allow ourselves to imagine and become excited, it brings us focus and a determination that many others can lose.

I'm a great believer in dreaming. Any dreaming. Daydreaming, dreaming big, lucid dreams, recurring dreams, living your dreams. Just not nightmares, although in attempting to achieve your dreams, you better be ready for a few nightmares along the way. We'll deal with them later!

We should all be encouraged to dream big, really big. This is what got me through high school. This is what kept me excited.

Like many kids, my dream from a young age was to make it. Well, to be completely honest my dream was simply to be famous. Rock star, comedian, TV presenter, didn't really matter to me. I just wanted to be famous.

I realise now this is where many of the problems associated with dreaming lie. The concept of 'making it' has no real purpose or meaning to it. But this is a real problem with modern life; there's a fair few people out there building a life for themselves around just this, making it.

Where I used to watch people on TV and dream about being on there one day, social media has brought the concept of being famous to a whole new generation and presented it in such a way that it feels much more achievable. You now don't even have to leave your bedroom, all you need is a phone and boom, you've made it! Apparently. . . .

But as I got into my early teens the dream had already begun to take shape. From the age of 13, I was sitting in my bedroom writing scripts. At times it was all I could think about, I had dozens of notebooks filled with ideas!

I had one eye on going to university as this was what was expected of me and one eye set firmly on the world-famous Edinburgh Fringe Festival, the most legendary comedy festival in the world. A place some of the biggest names in entertainment 'made' it.

This all stemmed from my obsession with comedy as a kid. In particular, sketch comedy.

All through my teens I couldn't stop watching comedy sketch shows. But not your average run-of-the-mill, Saturday night mainstream shows. The stuff I was watching was different from the norm. Off-the-wall, surreal comedy. Crazy characters, wacky costumes and just pure silliness. I was drawn to them. I had no idea at the time, but I realise now that it gave me a sense of escapism.

Surely I could do what they do? Them and me, weirdos together.

It felt like I'd belong in their world; I'd lie in bed every night playing it out. In my mind I had found the perfect career. And although I had zero idea of the work required, the time, energy and dedication needed, there appeared to be a place for me in the world after all.

Others' opinions were not always so positive.

I went through my teens in the 90s. It might look terrible to you but the 90s were awesome, especially if you wanted to be in a band. Don't get me wrong, I love music, I especially loved music in the 90s and if I could sing or play a musical instrument, I'd absolutely have formed a band. And in my mind we'd have been great. Yup, I've thought about it long and hard, we'd be called Sweet Brioche.

But, if you wanted to write, to perform sketch comedy, wear silly dresses, beards, wigs and put on silly voices . . . not so acceptable. It wasn't cool, *yet*. You know how judgemental teenagers can be. So, I kept it to myself. I told very few people that I was going to go for it. But this is the key part, I *was* going to go for it. I may only have been a young teenager, but I knew. Having played it out thousands of times, I could see it in my mind.

But imagining it and doing it are two different things. You need both parts. I had nailed the first.

'The world needs dreamers and the world needs doers. But above all, the world needs dreamers who do.'

—*Sarah Ban Breathnach*

This is the bit that really interests me about having a dream. Why do some dream about something but then do nothing about it? And why do some dream about something and do everything to make it happen? The latter might not succeed but they'll do everything they can to try. Perhaps that's why the former doesn't pursue their dream; maybe the fear of failure is enough to put some of us off? Perhaps it's the fear of what others will think?

I worried about what others would say and think, but the desire to live my dream was greater. I needed to 'make it'. Whatever that meant. . . .

So, I decided to give it a go.

Now, for the purposes of 'scene setting', I need to share a little of my comedy journey with you. It's not a case of 'hey readers, check out what I achieved', it's more a case of **'hey readers, check out the awesome adventure I went on where I totally nearly made it but totally didn't make it, and it hurt for a very long time, but years later as I put things into perspective, I realised I totally did make it . . . just in other ways.'**

That last sentence may be a mouthful and not make good grammatical sense, but I hope you get the gist of it?

Ok, stay with me. . . .

'You really don't want to be famous. Read the biography of any famous person.'

—*Kevin Kelly*

My first Edinburgh Fringe was way back in 2000 as one half of a double-act known as Gav 'n' Rolls. Rolls was my best friend, the best friend I ever had. We grew up together, inseparable and with a shared love of all things silly. Rolls is to this day the funniest human I've ever met in my life. There is no one else in the world that has made me laugh as much as this guy. To make it even better he also has a beautiful soul. One of the good guys.

We were in our late teens and had absolutely no idea what we were doing. No performing experience, no background in theatre and no showbiz parents who had been there before us. But we went for it. Days spent writing and rehearsing. Hours and hours spent pacing the cobbled streets of Edinburgh, handing out thousands of flyers to potential audience members, putting up posters, trying to convince even just one person to come and see our first-ever full hour of comedy.

There were no smart phones, so we didn't have the power of TikTok, Facebook or Twitter. This required us to turn up fully.

'You guys are doing comedy?' friends asked, regularly with puzzled faces.

We had no money and absolutely zero reputation, so we had to just get ourselves out there and give it everything we had. And at 3 pm every single day we took to a tiny stage in the corner of a basement, in a pub, in Edinburgh.

Our biggest audience that year was 36. Our smallest was 1. And we had 2 'no show' days as no one turned up.

This hurt. A lot.

We kept going.

Of course, we didn't live in Edinburgh and had nowhere to stay for the month. The plan was to ask people in the audience each day if they wanted us to live with them, for free, for four weeks. This was either crazy or genius. And in the meantime, we had Rolls' mum's car and two sleeping bags as back up! We also had huge belief in humanity and on day one, among our huge audience of 11 we met Grant and Polly, who not only enjoyed our show but offered us a place to stay.

This blew our minds. They enjoyed *our* show *and* asked if we wanted to crash at their place! Friends for life and we still owe them both big time.

How awesome are humans? I mean, they could've been mass murderers but thankfully not!

Our first Edinburgh Fringe was incredible. In some people's minds it was a massive flop, a huge failure. Barely anyone turned up and we didn't make a penny. No one wrote about us, and no one got excited. No one cared.

Except us.

I mentioned earlier that everything boils down to thinking. We have a choice, always. We chose to see our experience as a success. We chose to get excited. We chose to care. We chose to learn.

We were just so grateful for the whole experience. We stood at the door after each show and thanked every single audience member for coming as we shook their hands. We mixed and performed with many other new acts, some of whom have gone on to become household names.

And that's part of the lure of course, you *might* make it. Every year there's two or three acts whose stars align and it happens. Sometimes on a scale that many only ever dream of. And that remember, had always been my dream.

To make it. Again, whatever that even means.

But that's just it. *Everyone* in the performing world is a dreamer. We're all dreaming of the same thing. Packed out venues, queues all the way down the street, roars of laughter, five-star reviews and rubbing shoulders with your heroes. And if you work hard, give it everything and don't act like a dick then it **might** actually happen.

*Note: In life some proper dicks do make it, unfortunately, and some proper good people turn into massive dicks too.

We put ourselves out there, taking on every gig we could, travelling the length and breadth of the country, sharing our minds with anyone who would listen.

In a short space of time it took us around the world. In 2002, we completed a successful run at the Melbourne International Comedy Festival in Australia. Things were getting real. The dream was coming true. This was it.

Except it wasn't it.

After a year living out of a suitcase, performing at some of the biggest festivals in the world, for so many reasons that I still don't fully understand, it all came to an end.

It was over.

 For the first time in my life, I felt down. Like, really down. I'm very reluctant to use the word 'depressed' here because I didn't seek professional help and it's not a subject to mess about with. But I was depressed. I know that now but at the time as I lay in my bed crying myself to sleep every night, I didn't have a clue what was wrong with me. I just put it down to being very sad. I was so sad I smelled of sadness. This had been my dream since I was 5 years old. And it was over. Gone. And my best friend in the whole world had decided on another path. Like all good double acts, we drifted and this was the hardest part. The constant focus on 'making it' had ultimately driven a wedge between me and the most important friend I've ever had.

I found myself in my early 20s and the fun had gone. Life felt kinda rubbish.

In 2003, I decided to get a job at the Edinburgh Fringe working for legendary theatre company Gilded Balloon. I figured it would allow me to keep a 'foot in the door' of the comedy world. They put me in charge of running 'The Caves', a venue that would go on to mean more to me than any other venue in the world. Gilded Balloon had dozens of shows on in 'The Caves' that year but two in particular will stick in my mind forever.

Stick with me here reader, there's some key learning coming up. . . .

Firstly, I want to mention 'Slaughterhouse Live'. They were on in the 'Big Cave', a venue that is quite literally a cave. It holds 150 people and has an extraordinary atmosphere. This show inspired me and my comedy more than any other show I've ever seen at the Fringe.

'Normality is a paved road: It's comfortable to walk, but no flowers grow.'

—Vincent van Gogh

Five guys working together to create a world that was entirely their own. Clever, silly, surreal and utterly hilarious. Still to this day the best and funniest show I have ever seen. It was very Gav 'n' Rolls. High-energy, in your face humour. Why they didn't have TV execs queuing up to sign them I'll never know.

With Gav 'n' Rolls having come to a very difficult end, 'Slaughterhouse Live' is the one show that picked me up and gave me the belief that one day I'd have my chance once again. Maybe one day I'd play the 'Big Cave' to a full house like them. I was for the first time in months feeling inspired again.

Secondly, a fairly new act called 'Flight of the Conchords' were also playing the big stage in 'The Caves' that year. I saw something happen that year that blew my mind. Right from the start, these two guys from New Zealand had a packed out venue, queues all the way down the street, five-star reviews and some of the biggest names in comedy clambering for a ticket and in some cases (a very famous TV comedian who will remain nameless) *desperate* to be their friend. It was very clear to me that 'Flight of the Conchords' would go on to become a global phenomenon. I saw it happen. It was possible but couldn't be further from what I had experienced just a few months earlier with Rolls.

But the thing that struck me the most about both 'Slaughterhouse Live' and 'Flight of the Conchords' was not the fact their shows were great but the fact they were/are such nice guys. All of them. Down to earth. Lovely. No ego. A delight to talk to. Helpful. Encouraging. Who better to spend a month in a cave with?

The other thing that appealed to me was the fact they were in it together. 'Conchords' a double act and 'Slaughterhouse' a five piece. Each act a team. Bouncing ideas off each other, sharing the highs and of course the lows. A true connection, a friendship. No one better than the other.

How do you find that in others? The types of people that it all just clicks with, when it's just meant to be. I'll say it until the day I die, Gav 'n' Rolls had it. We could've and should've been huge. But whilst we had some unbelievable times it simply wasn't meant to be. It took me over 10 years to accept that.

10 years.

But I learned that, just like people, dreams can change. Dreams do change. Sometimes – again, like people – they must. And that's ok.

Fast forward to Edinburgh Fringe 2012. I had thrown myself back in for a second crack. Along with a magician and a mindreader I was now part of a three-piece act known as 'The Colour Ham'. A sketch magic show. A what?! I hear you ask! Three very different performers from very different backgrounds creating something entirely new.

On paper our show simply should not have worked.

Our show was rejected by all the major Fringe venues except one, 'Just the Tonic', who took a punt. Due to other commitments, we could only commit to the first eleven nights. It just so happened they had a slot available for those eleven nights. At 9 pm. In 'The Caves'. 'The Big Cave'. THE BIG CAVE. It was like it was meant to be and although this time we knew a little bit more about what we were doing, we were still winging it.

'The Colour Ham' went on to play the 'Big Cave' three years in a row at the Fringe. We had a packed venue, sold out pretty much every night, won awards and performed for the BBC.

It had taken me 10 years.

'They came out of nowhere,' said one reviewer.

10 years.

don't give up.

don't give up.

don't give up.

don't give up.

don't give up.

don't give up.

don't give up.

don't give up.

don't give up.

don't give up.

There were queues all the way down the street, five-star reviews and we rubbed shoulders with our heroes. We had the team, the connection, that thing that Gav 'n' Rolls, Slaughterhouse and Conchords all had. Everything I had dreamed of was coming true. Finally.

'I always did something I was a little not ready to do. I think that's how you grow. When there's that moment of, "Wow, I'm not really sure I can do this," and you push through those moments, that's when you have a breakthrough.'

—*Marissa Mayer*

I used to dream that one day people would write about us. I used to imagine 15-year-olds sitting in their bedrooms reading the reviews of *my* show, inspiring *them* to create *their* show.

I used to write imaginary reviews but now people were writing about us. They were writing things such as . . .

'They've conceived something quite special, and unlike anything you've seen before.'

'The thing that strikes me most about them is just how much they believe in what they're doing.'

'It's really exciting to catch something that rejects the status quo, and is proud to be completely unique.'

'These three are pioneering a new standard of funny, and forging something memorable; the sort of thing you'll tell your friends about.'

'Comedy is the new rock and roll, folks, and this band are on the verge of something great. See them while the tickets are still cheap.'

'These guys are going to be snapped up by TV execs any moment now!'

They saw it.

The dream was coming true.

And then guess what?

It ended.

Just as quickly as it all began.

Devastated.

Again.

In 2015, we performed for the last time ever together at the Edinburgh Fringe. This was to be our fourth and final Fringe together.

Three best friends having the time of their lives had become three colleagues vying for the centre spot on the posters.

Three incredibly close friends were now three distant and very busy acquaintances struggling to find the time for each other.

Three mates without a care in the world, going for it and following their hearts, now worrying about reputations and following their heads instead.

'Making it' seemed to have got in the way yet again . . .

Once again I found myself feeling very down. The smell of sadness lingered once more.

After years of performing live stand up, I find myself not involved these days. I've moved on to different things. Part of me is absolutely delighted. Stand-up is exhausting, stressful, difficult, and full of assholes. I'm able to go see other people's shows for a change and most importantly see my family.

But I can't lie, the other part of me is heartbroken. All those years working so hard to create something that made people laugh until they cried. One review wrote 'I laughed so hard I nearly shat.' I'm proud of this one.

Performing stand-up is exhilarating, it's magical, it's wonderful. Some of my happiest times were on stage at the Fringe with 'The Colour Ham' and I miss it. I miss performing. I miss the buzz. I miss being in that moment on stage with the team when you don't even need to say anything, you just know what each other is thinking. That moment when the audience know and you know that something really special is happening there and then between real friends and it's pure magic. I miss that.

I miss my best friends.

But I did it. We did it.

I gave it my all and we rocked out so much that people nearly shat themselves.

Most dreams are born in teenage minds, in teenage bedrooms. I was 5 when I first thought about being on stage but I was 13 when I picked up a pen and paper and really started to map it out.

All along the way I met the self-doubts, the knocks, the knockbacks, the judgements, the critics, the failures and the bullies. But the highs outweighed them all.

The challenge so many young people have is something called meritocracy. Now I'm not going to lie, I didn't know what meritocracy even meant until just a few years ago. So if I can paraphrase 'School of Life', basically, our societies tell us that everyone is free to make it if they have the talent and energy. We have it drummed into us from a young age that if we're talented enough and we have the passion then we'll make it, we can be anything we ever dreamt of being. Where this falls down, however, is if we fail or don't quite fulfil our ambition, well, then we must be a bit rubbish, lacking in talent or just lazy. This creates a divided society where those deemed to be the best must then be deserving of all their success, leaving the rest of us to be worthy of our rubbishness. Not just unfortunate, but losers.

When my comedy career came to an end – twice – this is exactly how I felt. But we weren't rubbish, we had talent and we worked damn hard. But we didn't 'make it'.

Or did we?

We maybe didn't 'make it' in the traditional sense. I didn't end up with my own TV show. I didn't make the movie and I didn't make millions and travel on a private jet.

But looking back, I realise I did make it. I made it big time. Years of excitement, fun, making people laugh, creativity, travel, making friends and creating the most extraordinary memories.

Yeah, I made it. And it has made me. I made me.

And you get to make you.

If you find yourself sitting in your room, allowing your thinking to wander, allowing your thinking to grow, daring to dream big, then no matter what your dream is, if you decide to go for it then give it everything. It might just lead to the most extraordinary adventure.

Maybe it won't work out. But maybe seeing if it does will still be the best adventure ever. It might all come crashing down around you but don't let it turn you into a dick and whatever you do, remember those who inspired you, remain thankful and always, *always*, remember your friends who were there at the start. One day you might just stop and realise you forgot all about the ones who cared.

And remember, dreams *can* change.

To new dreams.

" **If you sit on a shelf for the rest of your life, you'll never find out.** "

—Woody, Toy Story 4

CHAPTER 4

You Are Not Everyone Else

So Unfair!

When I was 13 there was a comedy show on TV called *Harry Enfield and Chums*. Enfield was one of the most successful comedians in the UK at the time and his sketch show had some of the most memorable character creations, many of which are still relevant to this day.

In particular, Kevin Quentin Julius Patterson. 'Kevin the Teenager' was the portrayal of life through the eyes of a teenager. In the first sketch Kevin's parents were horrified to discover that as the clock struck midnight on the day of Kevin's 13th birthday, he immediately forgot all his manners, his posture changed, his hair hung over his face, his room turned into a bombsite and life was all of a sudden 'SO UNFAIR!' He went to bed a lovely, kind 12-year-old and woke up a not so lovely 13-year-old who communicated mainly through grunting.

Kevin was always rude to his parents, frequently shouting 'I hate you, I wish I'd never been born!' He was unable to keep his room tidy, had an apparent allergy to hard work, thought a lot about sex, played loads of video games and like many teens he was heavily influenced by peer pressure and celebrity.

And whilst Enfield's creation was very much an exaggerated, caricature of teen life, so much of it rang true with me at that age. My dad would occasionally call me Kevin! I hated it but he wasn't far off.

One of things I always remember from the show was the idea that teenagers are always very polite to all parents except their own. Isn't it so true? I'm not suggesting you're not kind to your parents but it's funny how our best behaviour is often saved for other people's parents!

Basically, if Kevin is a true representation of teenage life, then the rules of being a teenager would be as follows:

1. All communication should be carried out via grunts, shrugs, and monosyllabic exchanges of 'No', 'Fine' and 'Why?'
2. Literally every single mug, glass and plate should be kept in your room, dirty.
3. Leave lights on. Always.
4. Bedroom carpets should not be visible, cover with clothes and towels.
5. Eat everything in the fridge, except green stuff.
6. Leave empty packets in the fridge.
7. Do not use any bin.
8. Don't sleep. And when you do, sleep in.
9. Slam doors.
10. Tut.
11. Drama. Often.
12. Don't fit in. And when you do, worry about what people think of you.
13. Roll eyes. Especially when your parents do anything deemed as 'trying to be cool'.
14. Say 'literally' a lot.
15. Blame your parents. For everything.
16. Be emotional but do not love yourself.
17. Know everything, even when you don't.
18. Feel self-conscious, all the time, for no reason.
19. Do stupid things.
20. Never put your phone down. Ever.

I'm pretty sure we could add a few more and while you may be able to relate to a few of these, you might also be thinking '*Ok Gav, I get it, I'm a teenager and the world sees me as a lazy, grumpy, hormonal pain in the ass.*'

Well, actually, that's not how the world sees you. The world sees teenagers as the future. As a creative, curious force. As potential. As hope.

Don't get me wrong, sometimes you're definitely a lazy, grumpy, hormonal pain in the ass but aren't we all?!

But you are incredible and while you probably make mistakes here and there, while you probably piss your parents off no end and while you really, really do need to tidy your room more, you're an extraordinary human, capable of making a difference.

Oh, and for those of you who worry about not fitting in, see the thing that makes you not fit in? Yeah, whatever the thing is, *that's* your wee piece of magic. Be proud of it. That's your extra in the ordinary. It's what makes you, you!

It's liberating when you finally accept that you are not everyone else and you don't need to be doing what everyone else is doing.

Being a teenager is never perfect. Being 6 was so much easier. At that age your responsibilities included running as fast as you can and laughing. And someone else was in charge of your hair. Let me guess, people have already stopped asking you what your favourite dinosaur is. What's that about? It's like they don't even care.

Have another look at the rules above, read them again. And break them. I dare you. Break them all, that's your job. Prove the world wrong and *never* be afraid of your own style.

But you know and I know, there are no rules to being a teenager, there's simply no such thing. But if there was a list of rules, I reckon they would look a little like this. . . .

Let's call them The Anti-Rules to Teenagering.

1. Don't be a Dick

'A dickhead makes everything about them.'

—*Gilbert Enoka*

To be, or not to be? That is the question. It's tough, right?

Not really, and yet it's an everyday struggle for so many.

When I was 19 years old, I got a holiday job working for a large well-known high street clothing store. We'll call them NEXT, because that's their name.

First day. I arrived suited and booted ready to make an impact. I wore my best shirt, my best trousers and my best shoes. I wanted to make a great first impression.

I arrived nice and early, met the team and was instructed that my first task would be to restock the men's shirts on the shop floor.

Perfect. Nice, simple task. Take the shirts out the box, slide them into the correct spaces on the wall ensuring that the sizes are in order. I can do this.

First shirt needed to be slotted into the lowest space on the shelf. To be clear, the lowest space was pretty much on the floor, about 2 inches above to be exact.

So, in order to put the shirt into the slot I would need to bend/crouch down to reach it.

I took the shirt, I bent down. My trousers tore.

I can still hear the noise.

Now, just to provide a little more detail here . . .

When I say they tore, I don't mean a little tear at the seams that goes unnoticed. I mean the biggest kind of tear that can't *not* be seen. The kind of tear that once you've seen it, you can't unsee it.

In simpler terms, there was a draft.

It was the kind of tear you simply don't have on view when working in a clothing store. Or any store.

This was bad.

First 5 minutes into the first day of a new job and my bum was hanging out of my trousers. I'm having a wee chuckle to myself as I write this but at the time it wasn't so funny. I kinda panicked a little. First impressions and all . . .

I hatched a plan.

Speak to the boss, do the right thing, tell her what's happened and provide a solution.

My solution was simple. Take a new pair of trousers off the rail in the store and pay for them. Or take it out of my wages. It makes sense, right? I'm working in a clothes store, they sell men's trousers. Easy.

The walk from the scene of the accident to my new boss's office would have made for great YouTube viewing. I had to cross the entire shop floor, weaving in and out of customers and clothing rails, trying my best not to reveal what had happened.

I pirouetted my way round the shirts, charleston'd through the suits, time warped past the shoes, YMCA'd under the belts, Beyoncé'd my way down the escalator, moonwalked, macarena'd and with a bright red face 'gangnammed-before-it-was-even-invented' my way into the boss's office.

'Gavin,' she said, 'How's the first day going?'

'Well, it's funny you should ask.'

She looked very serious.

'So, it's a little bit embarrassing, I've had a wee accident.'

Her stare hardened.

'But it's easily fixed.'

Her stare was now at headteacher level.

'So, you won't believe this, but as I put the first shirt on the shelf my trousers tore.'

She didn't even flinch.

Surely she should be laughing.

 Nothing.

'But I have an idea.'

Nothing.

'I'll quickly grab a pair of trousers off the rail and pay for them either today, tomorrow or you can take it out my wages.'

She raised an eyebrow, still no laughter, not even a tiny little side smile.

She began to speak . . .

'I have some safety pins. You could turn your trousers inside out and safety pin them. That will do the job I'm sure.'

I proceeded to have one of those moments where you aren't quite sure if the other person is being serious or having a joke at your expense because in this type of situation it fully deserves a joke. I was fully ready to have the mickey taken out of me and forever more be *that* guy!

So I did what we all do in those moments, I kind of pointed and smiled as if to say 'You're kidding right?'

Nothing.

In my mind I'm thinking 'This must be a joke. It's a clothes shop. They have trousers. I can buy trousers. I can wear my new trousers.'

Still nothing.

'So . . . I can't just go and get new trousers?'

'How about you just go home Gavin?'

'Eh! Really?'

'Yup. Take the day off and we'll probably just have you working in the stock room from now on.'

'Blowing out someone else's flame won't make yours shine brighter. Remember that.'

—*Anon*

'You're serious right? I've to go home and not just buy new trousers in the shop that I am currently working in? That sells trousers. For men. Here. In this shop right now.'

Nothing.

Now, you might be wondering why I'm sharing this story with you in this book. Where's the learning point, where's the big underlying inspirational message?

Well, it's this . . .

Some people are dicks.

Simple.

And in my story, my boss proved herself to be a dick. I was trying to be as professional about it as possible. It was an accident, a rather embarrassing one at that. But she chose to be a dick about it.

You see, the thing is I believe we can *all* be dicks from time to time. But I also believe we all know when we're being a dick. We just know, right? When you're being a dick there is a voice in your head telling you that you're being a dick. It's literally telling you you're being a dick.

We know not to be a dick but sometimes we're just dicks. So don't be a dick. If you know you're being a dick, stop it. She knew she was being a dick and yet she kept being a dick.

It's time for people to stop being dicks.

As Dr Seuss said,

'Be who you are and say what you feel because those who mind don't matter and those who matter don't mind.'

What should I say to her in this moment? There were many options. I said nothing.

I thought to myself, 'Don't be a dick'. I made the choice. So I wasn't a dick.

I smiled and I left.

I've always wondered if she watched the CCTV back after I'd left. If she did, she'd have seen some of the finest moves ever to be witnessed and she'd have realised I had skills she'd never even heard of.

And please remember, you're never too important to be nice to people.

2. You Don't Have to Make It to Make It

The desire to 'make it' is a popular dream. It pollutes teenage minds and bedrooms the world over. It's a hunger shared by millions. But what stipulates 'making it' and where does it end?

Is it fame? Having it all? A million followers? Whoever you are, being a rock star in every single area of your life is impossible and will bring you nothing but stress and pressure.

It won't end. Once you've started the chase, when do you stop? Your goal of 'making it' becomes a never-ending struggle with ever-changing goalposts. It will drain you of all your energy and over time your friends will be left wondering what happened to you.

I have very few friends. Don't get me wrong, I have wonderful friends but there's not many of them. Real ones anyway. I know for a fact there's people no longer in my life because I was simply too busy 'making it'.

To be able to say 'I've made it' at the expense of true happiness, friendship and love is one of life's great mysteries and yet it lures millions into its lifelong chase.

Instead of trying to 'make it', work out what 'making it' actually means to you. Is it to produce a body of work you are proud of? Is it to have a house? A family? To run your own business?

But is it the end result or is it more about the journey, becoming a better person, learning, making a difference, having fantastic experiences and being happy now? Work it out for the sake of your own mental health because the goal of 'making it' doesn't cut it and nor does it end. Ever.

3. There's No Wrong Path

In my teens there was always pressure to go to university. That was always the recommended path to success. Anything else was sold to me as a failure. You go to school, you pass your exams, you go to university, pass more exams, get a job, get married, buy a house, done. You are now a success.

Absolute nonsense. It's just not how it works. Here's my journey.

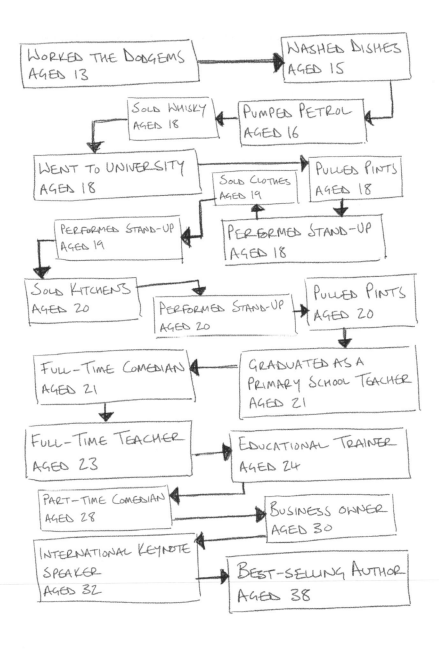

Remember, the fun is in the journey itself. There's no such thing as an overnight success!

4. Stop Saying Yes to Things You Hate

'If something is not a "hell, YEAH!", then it's a "no!"'

—James Altucher

Saying 'yes' is easy and your happiness is made up of the choices you make in life. That's quite a bold statement. But saying 'no' is a bold move. I'll say it again. Your happiness is made up of the choices you make in life.

We all know that being on the receiving end of a 'no' can be brutal. But you saying 'yes' to everything won't make up for that.

'No' is a complete sentence. It rarely requires anything after it. It can be used in any situation and it can, at times, feel wonderful.

But so often we feel the need to say 'yes'. Yes to our friends, yes to our parents, yes to our teachers, yes to the latest trends, yes to the latest gadgets, yes to someone else's plans at the weekend. . . . I could keep going.

And often when we really want to say 'no' we say 'yes' because it's easier than saying 'no' and then trying to justify why. We don't want to hurt anyone's feelings.

This just leads to feelings of regret.

I have recently set out to say 'no' more often. I had got to a stage in my life where I was finding I had less and less time to focus on the stuff that matters. I was a people pleaser. Now there's nothing wrong with wanting to please others and be of help unless it's at the expense of your own happiness. And that's exactly where I had got to.

I look back on my teenage years and I was the same. Sometimes I couldn't think of anything worse than going to a particular person's house or to a particular party, but everyone else was going and I didn't want to be the only one who wasn't. So, often I said 'yes'. I'd go and whilst sometimes I would be glad I went, more often than not I found myself wishing I had the confidence to say 'no'.

Saying 'no' is great, it's not a crime! Sometimes it's hard but you will have to say 'no' to many things in life in order to say 'yes' to others. Let's call it 'The Joy of No' or JONO for short.

I'm currently training for the London Marathon and I'm having to say 'no' to many things just now: late nights, alcohol and junk food to name just a few. But by saying 'no' to these things I'm saying 'yes' to getting fit and healthy.

As a teenager there's the obvious things that you are *absolutely* allowed to say 'no' to, such as sex, drugs and alcohol. And if your friends are quick to judge you negatively then maybe it's time to find some new friends!

But sex, drugs and alcohol aside, there are so many other things in life you can take great pleasure in saying 'no' to. Here's my #JONO top 10:

- Negative self-talk
- Perfection
- Excuses
- Comparisons
- Parties
- Unhealthy food
- Social media
- Bitching
- Terrible friends
- Your phone

Dear Parents,

More than anything in the world I want you to be proud of me. I adore you but right now I'm the most stressed I've ever been in my whole life.

Your teenager

5. Sidekicks Are Cooler Than Heroes

I was delivering a workshop in a high school in Scotland. There were about 100 young teenagers in the room.

I had asked a question that was swiftly answered correctly by one of the boys. I congratulated the young man on his correct answer and asked him his name.

'Shaw,' he replied.

'Shawn?' I asked.

Clearly the young man had spent his whole life so far correcting people and with a frustrated tone he replied, 'SHAW, not Shawn, no "N" Just Shaw.'

'I have never heard that name before, it's cool, I like it. What does it mean?'

In his broad Scots accent the young man replied with 'Am no tellin ye!'

'Do you *know* what it means?' I asked.

'Aye,' Said Shaw.

'So, are you going to tell me?'

'Naw,' said Shaw.

'You have to tell us now, the fact you're *not* telling me would suggest it has an *awesome* meaning,' I said.

'Am no tellin ye' was Shaw's response yet again.

'I wasn't for giving up'. 'I'll tell you what my name means if you tell me what Shaw means.'

'You go first,' said Shaw.

'Gavin means Hawk of Battle or Eye of the Hawk. Either way it's like a Superhero or a Superhero's power.'

Shaw and his pals seemed suitably unimpressed.

I piped up again, 'Right, your turn, what does Shaw mean?'

Shaw took a deep breath and sighed. He said nothing.

'C'mon, What does Shaw mean? Go for it!'

And with another sigh Shaw finally replied . . .

'Little Row of Potatoes.'

The room erupted into a mixture of laughter and clapping.

Another kid commented on the fact that 'Little Row of Potatoes' definitely wasn't a Superhero name.

You can imagine Marvel launching their latest comic book, 'Hawk of Battle & Little Row of Potatoes'.

'Little Row of Potatoes' is definitely 'Hawk of Battle's' very own sidekick, like Batman & Robin but with a touch more country.

At the end of the session, though, as the group were leaving the room, another one of the kids approached me and simply said, 'I've always preferred the Sidekicks. I'd rather be a Sidekick, they're the real good guys.' And off he went.

It got me thinking, have we got it all wrong? Do we encourage people too often to be the Hero? Should we? The focus is always on the Superhero, they're the star of the show. But is it right?

'Batman's the triple bacon cheeseburger we paid for. Robin's the garden salad that came with it.'

—*Wired Cosmos*

Is the negative attention often aimed at sidekicks justified? What if some of us are happy not being the hero?

We hear phrases from time to time like 'Not all superheroes wear capes'. Do we need to be superheroes? Let's think about it in comic book terms. . . .

The sidekicks story usually isn't based around violence. They introduce an alternate point of view. They bring a more human element to the story essentially forcing our central character to open up, display their more caring side and share their emotions. The Sidekicks also clean up the mess and are happy to step back when the glory is being awarded. They're loyal and often the reason our hero succeeds. They can also bring much needed comic relief!

I guess what I'm saying is that we don't all need to be the hero. We don't even have to *want* to be the hero. We can be quietly confident, quietly happy. And some of us are happy this way. We don't crave the attention or the limelight. We're happy to find our hero that we support, that we align ourselves with. And we're still one of the good guys.

Blogger **Swimmer963** makes a great point.

'Heroes need sidekicks. They can function without them, but they function a lot better with them. Maybe it's true there aren't enough heroes in the world. But there sure as hell aren't enough sidekicks trying to help them. And there especially aren't enough talented, competent, awesome sidekicks.'

Is it any different in real life? Some strive to be a leader, some make it, others don't. But what about those who are more than happy to *not* be that person? Of course, it's great if in life you do want to be head of school, the boss, the manager, the captain, the director, the CEO, the lead role, the hero who has their name up in lights. But it's just as awesome should you be happy where you are.

If you're reading this and all you hear from your friends and family is that you should be putting yourself out there more or going for that thing they want you to go for and yet you really don't want to because you are HAPPY. Then good.

Be the best version of you. The you that is happy to not be the hero. Be the best little row of potatoes you can be. Potatoes are never the star of the show but by god do they pull a meal together and warm yer belly.

6. Heroes Are Still Cool

The nineteenth-century historian Thomas Carlyle once observed that 'Society is founded on hero worship'. Now, whether you agree with this or not, based on my own experiences and observations I definitely believe that to this day society still strives to ensure those who embody the best values of our culture are held up as objects of admiration. Whether we get this right or not is a whole other conversation. I mean, just take a look at the news ffs.

Scott Labarge writes that we need heroes because 'they define the limits of our aspirations'. But, of course, we're all different and my idea of a hero will be very different to that of the next person. And if it's true that we define our ideals by the heroes we choose, then there's a good chance that you and I will be quite different with a very different sense of what human awesomeness actually involves.

'One day, whatever your age, you will stumble upon someone who will start a fire in you that cannot die.'

—*Beau Taplin*

My heroes involve rock stars (mainly dead ones), writers, rugby players, comedians and my parents. If yours is Donald Trump, Jesus or Kim Kardashian then it's very likely you and I will see the world a touch different.

But that's ok. Kind of . . .

My heroes have always been people I admire and wish to emulate. Their achievements, performances, scripts, lyrics, humour and stories gave me a sense of possibility. They helped me to define the limits of my aspirations. They made me feel excited, like there was a place in the world for someone like me. My heroes gave me hope and a sense of belonging. They still do.

Find your heroes and allow yourself to be inspired by them.

7. Turn Up and Take Part

Life tells us from a young age that it's the taking part that counts. I'm not sure if many people believe this to be true; for most, the winning is still a priority. In competitive sport I get it. It's absolutely about the winning. In non-competitive sports then I absolutely agree that we can play for fun, it's good for us, it's fun and it can be social.

As a business owner I also understand competition. I understand why companies want to be number 1. But I feel more comfortable working *with* others. Just a few years ago, one of our 'competitors' literally wrote a letter to every single one of our clients criticising our business, telling them they were wasting their money using our services. Who does this? This is wrong on so many levels but we'll go with 'professionally' and 'morally' for now. Their defence was 'Well, business is business.'

You have to laugh!

But let's just imagine it was true and it really is the taking part that counts. What if there really is room for everyone? What if – as long as we're all in it for the right reason – we can share the space and make a bigger difference, together? In the case above of our 'competitor', we both work in schools. We both want to help young people to be more resilient and create positive futures. What if I'm fully booked up and an enquiry comes in that we simply cannot fulfil, I was able to say to the client 'give these folks a phone, they're magic'.

I know there are businesses that exist who do this. But not many. And I understand you're only going to recommend others who you believe to be excellent. But I like the sound and feel of this. The reality is that, within life, for all the wonderful, purpose-led, values-driven individuals out there, there are just too many cliques and too many egos.

But what if it was different?

What if we didn't just reward winning? What if we paid more attention to the 'taking part'? The 'doing', the 'trying' or even the 'not winning'? The 'failing'?

I'm not a subscriber to the 'Let's not dish out medals on sports day as everyone's a winner' mentality. If you're the best then you should absolutely win.

But what if you're the best at being 4th? Imagine being 4th best in the whole world at something but you don't get anything for it.

Or the best at being crap at running? Should there be a prize for this? Ok, I'm being facetious (again) now but life is for taking part. Turning up, getting stuck in, involved. But you don't need to be the best. You don't need to win. We can, however, enjoy living, enjoy being 'in' rather than 'out'.

What about having the 4th best beard in the world? Never mind this 1st, 2nd or 3rd best beard nonsense, 4th best beard is where it's at.

Random, huh?

Read on. . . .

In 2007, I entered the World Moustache and Beard Championships. Yes, it's true, this is actually a thing that exists. Men (and occasionally woman) from all over the world spend years growing, shaping, taming, sculpting and moulding their facial whiskers and every two years they gather somewhere in the world to celebrate the best of the best.

I only found out by chance about the World Moustache and Beard Championships 90 days before the actual competition and decided to enter. But there was a problem. I didn't have a moustache or a beard.

So, without any egging on from anyone, I filled in the forms and let the growing begin. I entered a category called 'Partial Beard Freestyle'. Again, this is actually a thing.

I set myself the following challenge:

- No shaving for 90 days
- Style it the night before the competition
- Turn up

For 90 days slowly but surely my beard began to take on a life of its own and before I knew it, it looked like a giant loaf of wholemeal bread had made home on my face.

People laughed, others pointed. Occasionally I was met with shouts of 'Hey Chewbacca', 'hairy face' and my particular favourite, 'How many birds live in there?'

Games of 'How Many Things Can You Hide in Gav's Beard?' became a regular fixture. And just in case anyone is wondering . . . 17 is the record. Often, people would poke fun at my ever-growing facial forest of fuzz. I, however, kept on growing.

The 90 days dragged on . . .

On the eve of the World Moustache and Beard Championships I drove for 9 hours and, in line with the original plan, in my hotel, I styled my beard.

The initial plan had been to style my beard into the word 'beard' but I was concerned that because I was doing it in the mirror the result may in fact read 'bread'.

So a last minute change of plan resulted in an epic sweeping moustache/sideburn combo with an enormous chin-talon of awesomeness. Photos do exist.

I donned my kilt and headed off to represent Scotland in the most prestigious Moustache and Beard competition in the world. When I turned up, I couldn't believe how many other contestants there were. Over 300 beard growers from all over the world had arrived. Beards down to the floor, spikey beards, curly beards, even beards in the shape of London Bridge. Every single style, shape, size you could imagine and more.

Over the next three hours a strange combo of London Fashion Week and Crufts for humans proceeded to unfold and 2,000 people turned up to watch. Yes, 2,000 people left their homes to look at beards and moustaches.

My name was called and I took to the stage, my facial masterpiece receiving thunderous applause.

That day I came 4th in the world. You will rarely meet anyone else in life who has achieved such a thing.

Throughout this story you have probably been wondering why on earth I or anyone else would have given the time and energy to such a bizarre undertaking?

It's simple.

Because I can. I wanted to take part.

It may be a bit different from the norm, but hey, normal is boring, right? It might be a bit weird, but hey, weird is also exciting, right?

It's no different to why people play football, sing, dance, draw, build and so on.

Because they can.

You don't even have to be the best but you can still be a part of something. You can still compete. You can still have fun.

It's amazing when you find something that's your thing. Something you can get into and be bothered about.

And who knows, you might even come 4th in the world.

'If you are not in the arena getting your ass kicked on occasion, I am not interested in or open to your feedback. There are a million cheap seats in the world today filled with people who will never be brave with their own lives, but will spend every ounce of energy they have hurling advice and judgement at those of us trying to dare greatly. Their only contributions are criticism, cynicism, and fear-mongering. If you're criticizing from a place where you're not also putting yourself on the line, I'm not interested in your feedback.'

—*Brené Brown*

8. Give a Shit

Giving a shit is for life, not just for Christmas.

But, we've not got an unlimited amount, and we need to direct them to the stuff that truly matters. We must give them. And we must get better at it.

Look at the world right now. There is simply not enough being given. The whole planet appears to be doomed for the very reason that some people simply don't have any more to give.

I can tell you right now, proudly and unapologetically, I give a shit. About me, my health, my family, my friends, my work, my whole life and the planet. I don't claim to be an expert in anything, I'm not particularly skilled at anything, but the journey that life has taken me on is simply down to the fact I care about making a difference. I want everyone to be happy.

This is very simple. You either care about you and your life or you don't, there's no in between. There are many things in this world that you can take great pleasure from ignoring. You don't *have* to care about everything in the world if you don't want to.

Maybe I care about too many things, maybe I overthink too many things, maybe I just care too much. But maybe that's my thing. . . .

Trust me. Identify all the magical things in the world, the stuff you're passionate about, that give you purpose and give all the shits you have to give.

9. Ask for Help

'In the beginning of life, when we are infants, we need others to survive, right? And at the end of life, when you get like me, you need others to survive, right? But here's the secret: In between, we need others as well.'

—Morrie Schwartz

Perhaps, more importantly, accept it. You don't have to be the one that does it all; start accepting you're only one person. Once you get it in your head that you are worthy of the luxury of having help from others, your world will open up, allowing you more time to do things that inspire you and, subsequently, those around you. And perhaps, more so, we need to get better at accepting help. It doesn't make us weak, in fact it's quite the opposite. It makes us stronger. Better even, at being human. And we need more of this.

'By reaching out, more comes back than you can possibly imagine.'

—Christopher Reeve

10. Don't Look the Other Way

I read a book recently about trees. Yeah yeah, I know, rock 'n' roll!

But check this, I found out that there's an underground network of roots throughout forests. Trees respond to their 'neighbourwoods' being cut or threatened. They sense which tree is cut and share roots in the earth to give water to those cut trees. They know!

Maybe you can tell I'm writing this having been awake since 3 am but I'm pretty sure there's some serious learning for humans in this. . . .

Kindness matters. Fairness matters. It's simple, we know when wrong is being done. Too many people in this world have become comfortable with looking the other way. Just because someone is different from you, just because it doesn't directly affect you, it doesn't make it ok. Look out for others, give, care, don't look the other way and definitely be more tree!

11. Take 39 Minutes and 38 Seconds

I woke for the first time as a 15 year old. I could think of nothing cooler than having my birthday on a Saturday. Well, there was one thing cooler and that was having your 15th birthday on a Saturday *and* getting a brand new Sony Walkman (Google it!). I also received a gift voucher for HMV. I threw on some clothes and headed for the train station, headphones round my neck, Walkman tucked in my pocket.

Half an hour later, with no idea what I was going to buy, I walked into HMV and I was drawn straight to one particular album. I can vividly remember the moment I picked it up in my hand, it was meant to be. I made my purchase and left the shop.

I had bought an album I'd never heard of by a band I'd never heard of. I liked their name, Green Day, it sounded weird. I liked the album title more, Dookie. Interesting word, Google it. . . .

Upon exiting HMV I made the decision to make my way home by bus, something I had never done. The bus takes 55 minutes, the train takes 15. It's a no-brainer, train wins hands down. However, for whatever reason, the bus was to be my birthday carriage home. I got on the bus and with no one else to be seen I sat down. I slowly tore the cellophane wrapper from my new purchase, popped the album into my Walkman, popped my headphones on and pressed play.

That was it.

For the next 39 minutes and 38 seconds I was transported to a place I'd never been before and from the opening riff my life changed forever. I was 15 years young and ready to take on the world. That sound, those lyrics. The hairs on the back of my neck stood, I felt an inexplicable rush of adrenaline and in just under 40 minutes I could see and feel all my dreams coming true. All my worries just seemed to vanish. The weight of the world which I wore around my neck gone. Never before had I felt so motivated in life, so energised, mobilised. Alive.

Happy. Truly happy.

I believe everyone has *that* album. The one that changed their life and if it's not an album then it's a film or a book or a show or maybe even a person. One that brings hope, energy and big ideas into their lives. One that ignites that giant fire in our bellies. One that makes us feel invincible.

That album didn't just open my mind up to a particular genre of music, it opened my mind up to believing that dreams can come true.

'To do something that you feel in your heart that's great, you need to make a lot of mistakes. Anything that's successful is a series of mistakes.'

—*Billie Joe Armstrong*

The power of music. The power of lyrics.

The opening track for *Dookie* is an anthem for the apathetic and un-interested outcasts. Its lyrics are a direct ode to indifference. What I heard was a young wannabe wanting to stay young and immature forever, someone who doesn't want to face the reality of growing up. The difference between him and I, though, is that he was prepared to drown in all the pressures that come with adulthood and accept the inevitable passing of time. I wasn't. I'm still not. I still try and do everything I can to stay young and immature. The world tells us to grow up. I consciously try my best to *not* feel like I'm growing up. Some would argue I am in fact growing down!

Then came track 2, 'Having a Blast'. I very much heard this song as a metaphor for bottled up emotions and anxiety. Don't worry, this is not just a track by track run down of an album but this track along with track 5, 'Basket Case', really spoke to me. Again, all about anxiety. At 15 years of age, I was the world's biggest worrier.

I worried about planes crashing, cancer, girls, rejection, boys, death, girls, bullies, weight, girls again and well, more death. I worried myself sick, literally. Very few people knew about my anxiety as a teenager.

It's important that I share this with you as I want you to know who I am and what it means to me to be able to write what I'm writing. I've spent much of my life as simply a scared wee boy from Scotland. And guess what? I still am. I'm still that wee boy at heart but from that day aged 15, I changed my mind about life. Well, to be more accurate I changed my mindset towards life.

That album put me on a new path.

I was a dreamer. Always had been. I had often heard the phrase 'Get your head out the clouds and stop dreaming Gavin'. I made a real effort to focus in school, to really hear what was being said and taught. Sometimes I was successful and other times not so much. My ability to concentrate wasn't great. I still find it hard.

Many of us spend far too long contemplating life and all that goes along with it; thoughts, feelings or problems. Sometimes we just need to trust our gut instinct and go for it. I had a moment that day. It was time to get my head back in the clouds and start dreaming again.

Find your Dookie.

'Waking up to who you are requires letting go of who you imagine yourself to be.'

—Alan Watts

12. Silliness Is Good for the Soul

I'm not entirely sure there is such a thing as a work-life balance. You wake up in the morning and you go to sleep at night. Everything in between is life. In saying that, slogging away for hours on end, continuously adding to your 'to-do' list, burning yourself out just to pay the bills isn't good for anyone.

Life can get serious. Finding reasons to laugh, lighten up and welcome some nonsense into your day is not only important, it's damn good for you. There is a whole science behind silliness but there is no science to actually being silly. Show Serious the door and welcome her distant cousin Silly in with open arms.

Research shows us that adults only laugh on average 17 times per day. That's 1.4 laughs an hour. There is an old-school, urban legend that tells us children laugh 300–400 times per day. Now, who am I to diss this, but all I'm saying is that if it's true then based on being awake for 12 hours children would be laughing at least once every 1–2 minutes from sunrise till sunset. True or not, it's fair to say, however, that little kids definitely laugh more than us.

13. Re-do Your Regrets

Forgive yourself for all the things you didn't do. Sounds easy but we all know it's incredibly difficult to do. Regret hurts every day. I used to spend months living in the past, feeling sorry for myself. Then someone introduced me to 'Re-do's'.

Choose the past memory that's hurting you the most. Imagine you could go back and do it all again. Write down how you would have done things differently and, in doing so, allow yourself to pick out and embrace all the key learning points. This allows us to affirm that we have learned a lot more from our past mistakes than we realised, and that if we had the skills we have now, back then, we would have done things differently.

Now I ask myself, 'What if I had never even tried?' This is followed by so many positive, beautiful answers. So much so that I can look back with nothing but love.

Everything in life is impermanent. We must remember to appreciate everyone and everything in the moment, at every stage.

'Life is like a sewer . . . what you get out of it depends on what you put into it.'

—Tom Lehrer

14. Quit Hitting Snooze

My dad used to tell me that a long lie-in was a wasted day. I'm sure we can agree that this is a little unfair and from time to time a long lie-in is pure bliss.

Getting up early can suck, especially mid-week. But one thing I have never done is hit snooze. Genuinely, I've never done it. My alarm kicks off and I get up immediately.

Most people will hit the snooze button at least once to prolong the inevitable exit from their warm bed. I get it. But I've always thought that if I'm hitting snooze over and over again then I clearly don't have enough things lined up in my day to excite me!

But there's actually some pretty hardcore reasons to stop hitting snooze.

It causes confusion for your body and the more you do it the less the quality of your sleep, and we all know we need sleep! Ask yourself why you're having to snooze your alarm in the first place.

Are you going to bed too late? Are you exercising? Are you scrolling too much before bed? Have you got a decent mattress?

It can be so hard to get out of bed. So what's the answer Gav?

Just get out of bed. That's it. You hear your alarm, get up and go smash your day.

15. Make Your Bed

I know, I know! Just those 3 words make you roll your eyes.

'If you want to make a difference in the world, start by making your bed.' There's a random yet bold statement to make. That was the premise of a speech delivered by Admiral William H. McRaven at the University of Texas at Austin in 2014. It has since gone viral with over 10 million views and has been referred to by some of the world's most successful people.

Until I was about 24, I almost never willingly made my bed. My dad used to tell me every day as a young kid and as a teenager. . . . *'Make your bed, it's important!'*

Important? I hated it, I never understood my dad's way of thinking; what's the point when I'm just going to get back in it? But now I'm a bed-making fan, mainly because it makes me feel good.

But get this, making your bed can actually make you happier and more productive. Weird, right? A survey from OnePoll and Sleepopolis found that people who make their beds regularly tend to be morning people who wake up without an alarm. They also tend to be more adventurous, sociable and confident. Rumour has it they're also more high maintenance, but we'll ignore that one.

Actually, all joking aside, I tend to have the personality traits of the non–bed makers: I can be a little socially awkward, anxious and definitely lacking in confidence.

However, I like it. It looks better, it helps me to get my day started and it just makes me feel happier.

'If you make your bed every morning, you will have accomplished the first task of the day,' McCraven explained. *'It will give you a small sense of pride, and it will encourage you to do another task, and another, and another. And by the end of the day that one task completed will have turned into many tasks completed.'*

Can having a neatly made bed really give you a sense of accomplishment?

'If by chance you have a miserable day, you will come home to a bed that is made – that you made – and a made bed gives you encouragement that tomorrow will be better,' McCraven added.

I love this! It might sound a bit weird or far-fetched, but I get it. Coming home to a messy house or a messy room after a long day or a tough day doesn't feel nice.

McCraven also says that **'Making your bed will [reinforce] the fact that the little things in life matter.'**

So basically, he's saying that If you can't do the little things right, you'll never be able to do the big things right.

I like it.

There's no doubt about it, making your bed is rubbish. So, why take the time to do it?

- You'll walk out of your room knowing you've achieved something.
- Build mental discipline; it's the last thing you want to do but it feels great when you do it anyway.
- According to the National Sleep Foundation, you'll probably sleep better.
- It builds better, healthier habits.
- You'll enjoy it.

So, I dare you to make your bed every day for a month and see how you feel. Get the family involved too. Not to make your bed, that defeats the whole point and might be a bit weird.

It might just change your life!

16. Beyoncé Wasn't Built in a Day

In 2003, pop music's biggest stars descended upon Edinburgh for the 10th annual MTV Europe Music Awards.

A massive big top in the Leith area of the city popped up and became the centre of the music universe for the night with a galaxy of top stars.

An estimated one billion people in 28 countries watched the show, featuring performances by the likes of Beyoncé.

And I was there. And so was Beyoncé.

And Beyoncé.

One of my comedy pals wangled me the role of supervisor. What did this even mean? What needed supervising? Could it be the audience, the staff or better still, could it be the stars themselves?

Whatever it was, it was huge. They were paying me, and I was well and truly in.

Did I mention Beyoncé?

I was 100% up to the task. I can supervise superstars. Nothing was going to stop me. This could be the greatest job in the world, and it was being handed to me on a plate.

My instructions were clear . . .

Supervise the shit out of the event. There will be some serious 'names' there.

Oh, and wear black. All black. Shirt, trousers and shoes.

I had the trousers and the shirt but I didn't have black shoes.

I bought new black shoes. Simple. I went for the cheap ones, but they would look the part.

Then came the big night itself. I was tired. I hadn't slept at all the night before. Partly because I was excited but I had also bought a new bed recently that just wasn't cutting it. My back was killing me, but nothing was going to stop me from breaking into the industry.

Could this be the opportunity of a lifetime? This was the biggest night in music; impress all the right people and maybe, just maybe, I could have a dream career in the entertainment business. How could I *not* be excited? This was huge.

I arrived early to be told where my position for the night would be. Essentially, I was given an area. This included the arena itself and a small backstage area.

My job remember was to supervise. In other words, to stand for hours and keep an eye out for anything untoward.

*Fact: I have never typed the word 'untoward' before.

And stand I did. For hours before anyone even started to arrive. My back slowly began getting worse. But I was up for it, I could feel the excitement building around the venue, occasionally I'd get a quick glimpse of a mega star. Pink, Timberlake, Aguilera and the likes.

Thousands gathered. I could hear the noise outside, it was incredible. I couldn't wait for it all to begin; this was a once in a lifetime opportunity and who knows where it could lead.

Then came the turning point of my night.

As the thousands of excitable fans filled the room I began to feel some intense pains in my feet.

Now, we've all had blisters before. This was not just your average, everyday blisters. I'm talking enormous blisters. The ones that are so painful you can't even walk.

Blisters *and* a bad back.

This was unbearable. I had a decision to make. . . .

Suck it up, grin and bear it, push through like a champ?

Or

Be a total wimp, sneak away and get my shoes off asap?

There was one simple question. . . . What would Beyoncé do?

Would she allow the blisters to ruin her opportunity? Would she sneak away and get her shoes off? Would she moan and complain to her manager about her sore feet?

NAW.

She's **Beyoncé**. She can command over $1,000,000 for a 5-minute performance. She's cool and she goes by one name.

In this moment I stood tall and tried to channel my inner Beyoncé. I thought to myself, C'mon, do what Beyoncé would do. She'd break out her alter ego Sacha Fierce, seize the moment and own the whole damn thing.

My alter ego is probably way more Dave the Postman than Sacha Fierce.

You see, I'm not anything like Beyoncé. I'm Gavin Oattes from Troon, and I had to get my new shoes off as fast as I could and sit down. My feet were bloody killing me and were clearly about to fall off.

I received instruction at this point to move to the smaller backstage area. This meant walking.

Ffs.

I probably had to walk about 100 yards. Each and every step though was torturous. I made a noise as I walked. Phonetically it would be spelled as follows:

'Huuahyaohsshhh'

Say it out loud. In fact, say it out loud while limping and you'll get the idea.

I got to my next position.

There was no one else around. This was my chance. I could take my shoes off for a while and give my feet a break.

Just as I bent down to take them off the door opened and in came a group of people. I quickly stood back up; 'Huuahyaohsshhh' I said out loud. Everyone turned and looked at me.

The first thing I noticed was how small everyone in the room seemed. Then I realised who they were.

In the exact same space as me were the following. . . .

Kylie Minogue, Christina Aguilera and Justin Hawkins, lead singer of Darkness. Pop *and* rock royalty.

And then it happened.

The door opened and in came Beyoncé. The most famous and powerful woman on the planet. Sacha Fierce Herself.

And all I could think about was my damn feet. By this stage the pain had reached a whole new level. My feet were channeling their own Sacha Fierce.

This was my moment to say hello to these people, to become their new best friend, to launch my brand new career in celebland.

'Do NOT mess this one up Gav,' I thought to myself. Just turn, smile and say hello.

I turned, I smiled, and a blister burst.

My feet were on fire. I needed to take my shoes off. I couldn't. Not in front of Beyoncé.

Just at this stage I was radioed once again to change positions. I was to head back out to the arena.

I hobbled back to my original position with tears in my eyes and never saw Beyoncé again.

The night came to an end and I left.

I got on the night bus to head home. To finally sit down felt like a dream.

The bus broke down and I had to walk the last 3 miles.

I chucked my shoes in a bin and walked home in my bare feet, the cold pavement felt amazing on my burning soles.

I contemplated my experience.

Honestly? Dreadful. The music was dreadful, the venue was dreadful, the job was dreadful, my new shoes were dreadful, and my new bed was dreadful.

But what did I learn?

No matter who you are or where life is taking you, always buy decent shoes and a decent bed. If you're not in one, then you're in the other. It matters.

I also learnt I'm not Beyoncé and that I don't belong in her world.

I'm me. You are you. And that's ok.

CHAPTER

Forever Elsewhere

What Do You Meme?

So, this part of the book is a bit different. It's about phones and social media. You might be thinking this is just here to keep the parents happy.

Maybe.

Not going to lie, when I did my research ahead of this book, I asked hundreds of parents the following question: *If I was to write a book for teenagers and could only cover one topic, what would it be?*

About 90% replied, 'Social media'.

If truth be told, I had already decided that I can't write a book for teenagers and not even slightly address the whole tech/social/phone thing.

Why do you think 90% of parents want me to write about this?

Is it because they don't get social media? Is it because they don't understand the technology the way you do? Is it because they're old and grew up in a different time?

Maybe.

Guess what?

When I did my research ahead of this book, I asked hundreds of teenagers the following question: *If I were to write a book for teenagers and could only cover one topic, what would it be?*

About 90% replied, 'Mental health'.

Then I asked: What is the main thing in your life impacting on your mental health?

Almost all replied, 'Social media'.

'*Some poor, phoneless fool is probably sitting next to a waterfall somewhere totally unaware of how angry and scared he's supposed to be.*'

—*Duncan Trussell*

So let's go back to my previous question. . . .

Why do you think 90% of parents want me to write about this?

Is it because they don't get social media *but* know it's impacting on your mental health? Is it because they don't understand the technology the way you do *but* they know it's impacting on your mental health? Is it because they're old and grew up in a different time and *therefore* worry about the impact of social media on your mental health?

Probably.

And lastly, is it because they care about you, a lot?

Definitely.

Dear Parents,
You might think I'm more interested
in my friends or my phone than you
right now.
Correct, I am. But I have one eye
on you, I see everything you do
for me, and I love you the most.

Your Teenager.
xxx

Just to be clear, this book isn't written for parents and I'm not about to ask you to chuck your phone off a bridge, nor am I about lecture you in all that's bad about social media and all the terrible things it's doing to your brain, eyes, confidence, sleep and self-worth . . . let's be honest, you already know that.

Instead, I'm going to share with you some cool stuff that I think you'll find interesting. And if the result is that you're inspired to change your habits a little for the better, use your time a little more positively, ultimately putting your phone down a little more with the end result being that you feel happier, then I think we can all agree, this would be nothing but a good thing.

So, here we go. Asked for by the parents and indirectly requested by the teenagers, this is my technology chapter.

Well, it's kind of about technology, it also happens to be about time, habits and your mental health. All hugely important.

Oh, I should probably mention, I don't actually know a great deal about technology, so let's start by talking about legendary rock star, Freddie Mercury.

Obviously.

Open Your Eyes, Look Up to the Skies and See

Before we can get into this, I need you to do a little something for me. It will take you 21 minutes.

Grab your phone, jump on to YouTube and search 'Freddie Mercury Live Aid'. And watch. Watch all of it. It doesn't matter if you're not a fan of the music, the clothing or the picture quality, I need you to watch it all.

Do it now, from start to finish.

And as you watch this footage, I want you to have a think about what you're seeing.

That's it, really simple. Go!

21 Minutes Later . . . .

How did you get on? Did you watch it all?

But did you?

Firstly, I hope you enjoyed it. Personally, his performance blows my mind every time I see it. I actually detest one of the songs, but it just doesn't matter and anyway, this task wasn't about the music.

The main thing I want to ask you here is: what were your main observations throughout the 21 minutes? Have a good think about it, what did you notice? What stood out for you the most?

I get that it's hard to see beyond the performance, millions upon millions have been transfixed by this footage over the years. You might not be aware of this, but that very performance is widely regarded as the greatest live rock performance of all time! Pretty cool, right?

That's not why I wanted you to watch it, though. As much as I love Freddie, was there anything in particular you noticed about the audience? Anything different or unique about them?

Not a single phone among them.

Not one person trying to watch through a 3×2-inch screen.

Not one single person focussed on recording the performance to upload later.

All utterly in the moment, entirely engaged with Freddie, his performance, and the music.

'Someone will always be prettier. Someone will always be smarter. Someone will always be younger. But they will never be you.'

—*Freddie Mercury*

We don't see this very often these days. It's now considered rare to see every single person looking up, smiling, joining in.

Smart phones of course, didn't exist in 1985; they do now, and habits have shifted massively. That's what happens. New technology arrives on the scene and with it comes new behaviours.

Think about it: 100,000 people living in the moment. Nowhere else to be, either in person *or* in the virtual world. To quote Freddie, 'it's a kind of magic'.

But for those of you thinking, 'Alright middle-aged man, you've made your point and you've introduced us to some old man music in the process . . .', there's another key point here. And it's maybe the biggest point of all.

And it's this. . . .

It took you less than 10 second to search for, and find, the greatest live rock performance of all time. At the touch of a screen and in the palm of your hand, you've got Freddie Mercury with 100,000 people in the palm of *his* hand!

It really is a kind of magic.

You've basically got the whole world in your hand, accessible 24 hours a day. Technology is incredible. I love it, but it changes things, not just behaviours, it changes everything, forever.

I'm not a tech geek, I mentioned earlier that I don't know a huge amount about technology. I'm not particularly intelligent when it comes to tech and I certainly don't live in a house that's tech'd up to max with all the latest gadgets and gizmos.

But I'm impressed by it.

Just like I'm impressed by engineering. I don't necessarily understand it but I can still be impressed. Planes, for example. Show me all the science and breakdown all the workings of a plane and I'll be impressed. But I don't get it. There's no way such a thing can take off and carry hundreds of people *and* their luggage, that's just ridiculous. But it does.

And don't get me started on cruise ships, they're nothing short of a miracle!

I'm just not clever enough to fully comprehend it. Technology is truly incredible, at times life-enhancing, other times life-changing and of course it can be life-saving. If it falls into any of these categories, I'm pretty much all for it.

Tweettokfacegramming

Let's do something almost no other book out there does and look at why social media is good for you.

It offers us multiple opportunities to connect with other humans. Look at what happened during the COVID pandemic, screens and all the different communication platforms literally saved lives. It allowed people of all ages to keep in touch, reconnect, check in on each other, maintaining spirits during a terrible time the world over. I couldn't go see my mum for over a year, but Whatsapp and Facetime allowed us to see and hear each other regularly.

Our family and friends are just a click away. New friends are just a click away. Our heroes are now just a click away. The days of having to stand outside a gig or a theatre door just to shout 'I love you, can I have your autograph' are long gone. Now you just message them from the toilet. Perhaps don't tell them you're on the toilet. That's definitely creepy.

Hi Ariana, just wanted to tell you that your lyrics in 'Break Up With Your Girlfriend, I'm Bored' really speak to me. Anyway, thank you again, need to go squeeze this one out as my little sister needs a poo too and the upstairs toilet is broken. Love you, Gav x

Weird, right?

Social media educates us. Where else could you learn what noise a goat makes when eating Doritos? Seriously though, YouTube it . . .

It can appeal to every single aspect of human emotion. There are videos, support, and advice for pretty much any issue and problem you could imagine, much of which isn't available anywhere else. There are amazing tutorials for dads to learn how to do their daughters' hair (I'm still a bit rubbish at it), videos to teach us how to contour, mix music, cook, train for a marathon, overcome self-harm, come out to our parents, the list goes on. Literally anything and everything. Social really can be a place to turn for advice.

Dear Parents,

The internet plays a huge part in my life.

I've not completed it yet, it's **MASSIVE**, I have a long way to go but I can tell you this, it's way more positive than you think.

Kind regards,

Your Teenager

x

One of the many upsides to social is that it can provide great entertainment. It can be hilarious. I have sat on many an occasion and wet myself laughing at people getting frights, falling over and cats stealing things. Friends are forever sending hilarious memes, ridiculous things their mum has done or their gran swearing. There must be years' worth of entertainment out there.

One of my all-time favourite videos was filmed by my great friend Eddie. In the video his dad is reading an article about how in Scotland, many of our street signs, place names, etc., are being translated into Gaelic. The article highlights the fact that on occasion the translations have not always been correct, giving the signs entirely different meanings.

Eddie's dad is trying to share a particular example from the Isle of Bute, off the west coast of Scotland.

Instead of reading 'Welcome to the beauty of the Isle of Bute', it was revealed that for nine years, the sign has in fact proclaimed, 'Welcome to the beauty of Penis Island'.

He can barely get his words out for laughing so much. I must have watched it 500 times and still it makes me cry with laughter.

It can make us feel good. We all love to hear positive feedback and we all love a 'like'. We can seek advice from all walks of life on a range of subjects from which shoes to wear, right through to dealing with your parents' divorce.

And guess what? It can bag you a cracking job. Employers the world over need people who know how to work, engage with, and maintain an online audience.

But, no one remembers their best day of social media.

And it can't all be good, right?

One of the original TV commercials for mobile phones sold us the dream of a 'freer life'. Perhaps before SMART technology took over this is exactly what it gave us. But now? A freer life? Really? I have images of Superman wearing his medallion of kryptonite, struggling to move and fighting for energy and air. Drowning almost. Some might consider this a rather dramatic comparison, but I'm not so sure.

'SMART phones bring you closer to a person far from you. But it takes you away from the ones sitting next to you!'

—Anon

Nowadays, telecoms giants have cottoned on to this and offer us a chance to go back. Back to the once mind-blowing days of a cell phone that allowed us to simply make calls, send texts and play Snake. These once complicated yet now simple machines are once again on sale. Imagine that? Imagine being a teenager with no SMART technology in your hand.

Most teenagers want a SMART phone. In fact, some crave it. It's a must-have item. Many have told me they believe their life is better with one. It enhances their life.

But have you ever wondered how different your life would be *without* a SMART phone?

Finding NEMO

So, you might be wondering what a Disney movie has to do with a chapter all about phones and tech. Well, as you'll find out shortly, *this* NEMO is entirely different from *that* Nemo. It wasn't meant to be about the movie at all but then the more I thought about it, the more I realised *that Finding Nemo* has got an awful lot to teach us when it comes to life and well, phones. . . .

I love a good Disney and Pixar movie. They rarely fail, from the extraordinary animation and wonderful characters to the heart-warming stories and life-enhancing messages, they've got it all, and they're damn good at it.

Every single Disney/Pixar movie has the same award-winning ingredients . . .

- Hero
- Sidekick
- Villain
- Magic
- Transformation
- Music
- Love
- Risk
- Sacrifice
- Setbacks
- Happy endings

Look at the list again, it basically sums up the life of a teenager. Or life in general?

Movie favourites of mine include *Coco, Tangled* and *Onward,* but for this part of my book I want us to briefly turn our attention to our fishy wee hero, Nemo. You don't need to be a fan of this movie to not only see but *feel* it's profound takeaways.

Whilst Nemo is very young in this film, it's not a million miles away from the everyday life of a teenager. For example, Dad's a bit embarrassing and we know Nemo should be listening to him more but at the exact same time we know that Marlin (Nemo's dad) needs to just learn to trust his son more and discover life for himself.

Sound familiar?

Whilst the 'parents just want what's best for you' messages are strong, the biggest takeaways of all are around trust and letting go of the things that hold us back. There's a great moment in the film where Dory and Marlin are inside the whale and Dory is translating what the whale is saying.

> **'He says it's time to let go. Everything's gonna be alright.'**
> **'How do you know something bad isn't gonna happen?' replies Marlin.**
> **'I don't!'**

The whole film is essentially based on the idea of trusting that if we let go, all will be ok. In fact, the more I think about it the more I realise that there's actually quite a few of these movies built around the concept of letting things go.

All together . . . 'LET IT GO! LET IT . . .' I'll stop there.

In the film, Nemo disappears. In real life, one of the most horrendous, panic-inducing moments in life is when you are 5 years old, you're at the supermarket with your parents and you turn away for all but 10 seconds, only to turn back and realise your parents are no longer there.

As a parent, I can tell you there is only one thing worse than this and it's when you're in the supermarket – or any other busy place for that matter – with your child, you turn away for all but 10 seconds, only to discover your phone is no longer in your pocket. . . .

I'm joking, of course.

But let's be honest, the moment you think you've lost your phone is quite something, right? The tremor of terror that runs through your entire being, ripping across your chest, around your heart, through the stomach, and down into your legs. The blood instantly drains from your face, and you need to sit down and learn to breathe again.

Other than the supermarket moment above, there's not much to rival that feeling when you think you've lost your phone.

For all the fun and entertainment that our SMART phones bring to our lives, they have also delivered an abundance of new problems right to the doorstep of our psyche.

Years ago, around the early 2000s, psychologists talked about something called nomophobia; an irrational fear of leaving home without a mobile phone. Going back to being the child in the supermarket, it's kind of the same, similar to what they call attachment theory. Where we have a dependency on our parents at that age because they look after us and know how to feed us and so on, nomophobia is where we develop emotional dependency on the phone because it holds details of our lives, photos, memories, secrets, bank details, and so on.

But it's also the device that acts as a gateway to your social platforms. Research tells me it's FOMO that creates the most separation anxiety among teenagers. Apparently the 'Fear of Missing Out' on what's happening on Snapchat, Instagram, TikTok, etc., can leave you panic-stricken about not knowing what's going on socially; in other words there's loads of fun stuff getting posted and guess what . . . you weren't involved!

But you know as well as I do that FOMO is proper old. It was replaced years ago by a brand new anxiety faced by social media users known as MoMo (The *Mystery* of Missing Out), aka the paranoia that stems from your friends not posting anything at all. You start thinking, *are they having so much fun that they can't even share it?*

Seriously though, this is now a thing, invented by humans, for humans. The invention of the tech itself is extraordinary but it's like we can no longer function as normal human beings without it in our hands, so as a result we're inventing new and awful emotions for ourselves.

Apparently, it's about belonging, being part of a peer group. Fitting in is what humans try and do. Remember in PE, when you weren't picked first, or even 10th for that matter, or a party that you never got invited to?

It's that.

It all starts in the playground, it's just nowadays, eventually, the playground moves online.

It's hard to accept that humans have become so hopeless at socialising without screens that we are at a complete loss when information isn't provided for us online?

MoMo shouldn't even be a thing? Can we all just agree now to reject MoMo in our lives, it's not worth the energy.

There's even FOMOMO (Fear of the Mystery of Missing Out). The feeling that you are missing out due to a broken or out-of-battery phone.

And while we're at it, let's never engage with 'BROMO': the act of your friends not posting pictures of the party you missed, so as to avoid 'rubbing things in'.

Eh?

So, let me get this right, BROMO is when you're worried because your friends *haven't* posted pics of a party you *didn't* go to?

Wow, humans win the day again!

Then there's FOJI – the fear of joining in (the flipside to FOMO), based on the idea of opting out of Instagram, TikTok, etc. because you don't know what to post and/or you're afraid no one will follow you. Another great invention.

But wait, there's more . . .

SLOMO. Yes, SLOMO.

A.k.a. 'slow to miss out'. SLOMO happens when you've checked out of social media for the night and awake to find your Instagram feed riddled with other people's fun. Imagine the horror? Day ruined. Obviously.

But, before I introduce you to what I believe to be the holy grail of phone separation anxiety-related acronyms, let me share with you one that I not only love and appreciate but find myself getting better and better at each day; JOMO.

JOMO is the 'joy of missing out'. I first heard of this a couple of years ago and loved the idea of non-participation being something that we embrace, something that we relish, given half the chance.

Sometimes there's no better feeling for me than seeing pictures appearing online from parties or events that I've *not* gone to.

However, JOMO may have been called the next big trend a few years ago and while all of the above may have featured in your life at some point, I would like to introduce you to NEMO. And finding NEMO might just be the holy grail.

It's for those striving to find a middle path between FOMO and JOMO. One isn't healthy and the other is perhaps unrealistic. It's the balance between the two extremes, a way of reducing the frustrations, the negativity, the validation cravings and yet you're still able to keep in the loop to some extent, focusing on using these platforms for good in your life.

This is the real life finding NEMO, 'Not Entirely Missing Out'. It's a happier, healthier place to be, and it's totally achievable.

How?

By taking Whale's advice of course; letting go and trusting that all will be ok.

'So you're telling teenagers to take life advice from a whale, in a Disney movie, about a fish?'

Yes. Yes I am.

'So what exactly is it we should be letting go of, Gav?'

Well, it's funny you should ask. . . .

The Art of Letting Go

Letting go of things that hold us back is a real skill, and it takes practice. Social media has taken a whole bunch of things that have always plagued teenagers (and adults) and successfully managed to elevate them to a whole new ninja level of 'holding us back'.

These include my lifelong friend, self-doubt. Not sure if you've ever met them? Along with self-doubt you may also have met a few other pals of mine; judgement, perfectionism, non-friends, jealousy, bitterness, procrastination, fear, regret, worry and entitlement. Each one stands strong on it's own but together they form one almighty gang. And this gang brings us nothing but trouble.

Let's start with where much of this stems from, and I warn you now dear reader, it's a biggie; Comparisonitis.

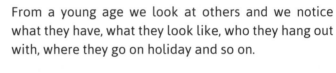

'Wanting to be someone else is a waste of who you are.'

—*Kurt Cobain*

Let's just all agree right from the off that it's hard *not* to compare yourself to others. It didn't start with the invention of social media. From a young age we look at others and we notice what they have, what they look like, who they hang out with, where they go on holiday and so on.

We're social creatures, we're primed to fit in, it's almost impossible at times to *not* compare our own lives to that of others.

Dear Parents,

Do you not think I'm doing enough comparing of my own in my own head?

I don't need you to tell me that someone else is better than me.

It hurts.

Have you not seen The Greatest Showman?

Kind regards,

Your Teenager

While comparisonitis may go back to the beginning of time, with dinosaurs walking the earth getting upset because Gareth the Triceratops had nicer shoes than everyone else, for me it was in high school that I really began to feel it.

Social media didn't exist then, but teenagers did. And so did the school yearbook. I looked forward to seeing the yearbook every year, thumbing through every page, exploring each and every sports team photo, best dressed teacher award, class picture and then of course the individual headshots, each one with their own humorous and carefully chosen words written below.

And do you know what I did? I worked my way through comparing myself to pretty much all of them. All I could see was how handsome/ pretty/weird/scary people were. A hair style, a smile, an item of clothing, the way someone was sitting. Our yearbook was basically just social media on paper, an early version of Facebook and once a year, all the social comparisons were compiled and published for all to see. Like an annual. It was the annual Comparefest.

At least no one could click 'like' or leave a mean comment below the photos.

I don't mind telling you that I would sit there thinking 'Look at that weirdo.' 'I wish I looked like him.' 'Who's that?' 'He's a bully, why do all the girls like him?' 'I wish she knew who I was.' 'His gran clearly cut his hair.' 'She's a dick.' 'Who wears that?!' 'I hate them!'

And on it went. But of course, it was all done with innocence, I had no idea what social comparison was. And perhaps more importantly, I kept it to myself. . . . I'll come back to this particular point shortly.

As Umair Haque tells us, social comparisons are 'me-versus-you' interactions, not 'me-with-you' or 'me-and-you' interactions. And so, I was projecting my fears, shortcomings and inadequacies.

But of course, you get to know people much better as your high school years roll on. It wasn't really until I left school that I realised how wrong I was about some people at my school. Some that I considered mates were in fact just narcissistic arseholes and some that I considered 'uncool' or 'not my kind of person', well, it turns out they were the coolest of all.

As for me, well, I've no idea what people thought of me, but I can tell you they were probably wrong. Very few knew the real me at school. I've already told you I did everything I could to fit in with the 'in crowd'. If that meant pretending to be someone I wasn't, then guilty as charged. It's tough being a teenager sometimes.

The in-crowd doesn't even exist. Well, it does . . . in *their* heads! I learned a long time ago that there's no such thing as an 'in-crowd' and if anyone out there believes they are part of a social group that are better than any other group of humans simply because of the way you look or where you're from, then you can piss off.

And then Mark whatshisname from Facebook came along and changed the social comparison goalposts. He gave the world a gift. The gift of a never-ending, modern day, high school reunion from hell.

'Simply muting and blocking common sources of "this makes me feel bad" and asking yourself "is this helping me or anyone", can help you streamline your experience in a positive manner.'

—Dr Ben Janaway

No longer was this an annual thing that appears in a book, but a daily one that appears in the palm of our hand. No longer just one picture to look at but EVERYTHING. Hours spent scrolling, clicking, looking and, of course, comparing.

And then the floodgates opened with Twitter, Instagram, Snapchat, TikTok, etc. etc. . . .

I've said it in previous books and I'll say it again, social media can make me feel unwell. It makes being peers difficult. Not just for teenagers but all of society. It can be a horrible place to be.

It's safe to say we now well and truly live in the age of envy and thanks to the invention of social media there's now an envy for everything. And there's levels!

'It's better to be real than perfect.'

—Anon

Magazines (remember them?) are definitely responsible for introducing the world to the basics of envy, Level 1: face, body, clothes and hair.

Facebook brought us Level 2: house, holiday, dinner.

Instagram moved us to defcon Level 3: everything at once.

Now we have school envy, bedroom envy, family envy, food envy, eyebrow envy, 6-pack stomach envy, cat envy, phone envy. You name it, there's an envy for it.

Many of us sit, engrossed in the slimming, hugely filtered #OutfitOfTheDay pics, and we want that body, that face, that tan, that outfit, that boy/girlfriend, that way of life. Even though we know it's not real, even though at a *logical* level we all know that images are filtered, and that people are presenting the very best take on their lives, on an *emotional* level, it's still pushing our buttons.

And before we know it, our own lives become a dazzling, flawless charade. Very few people show the real life side of their lives on social. We have millions the world over trying desperately to prove their life is just a good as they pretend it is online.

Social media has taken envy to an extreme with millions posting a daily 'best of'.

You see, we're taught to be the best, do our best and always be proud of who we are. But often what we post isn't a true reflection of who we are.

While psychologists often tell us teenage girls have it worse than most, no one is immune from it.

So why do we feel the need to post, share, scroll and compare?

Human beings look around at what everyone else is doing . . . *and copy*. As William Deresiewicz rightly points out, we've become the world's most excellent sheep.

The problem with social media is that we might be copying the *wrong* behaviours.

That awkward
moment when
the internet
goes down and you
don't know what to
do with your life.

Finding DORY

Just in case you've been living under a rock this last few years, *Finding Dory* is the superb sequel to *Finding Nemo*. It's not often sequels get it right but this one is superb. Dory is a very optimistic and kind, but a ditzy and forgetful fish. This is because she suffers from short-term memory loss. However, she has a heart of gold and is willing to go to great lengths to help those she loves.

It's a lovely film and like its predecessor has so much to offer when it comes to life and how we see the world. Or perhaps, more importantly, how the world sees us. It's rammed full of life lessons that apply to us all, lessons that truly make a difference. All of which we already know but perhaps in this modern social media-led era, like Dory, we've forgotten. Maybe we spend so much time now wrapped up in the 'Unreal' world that we've forgotten just what's important.

For me, there is 5 big takeaways in this movie that we all need to be reminded of sometimes:

- **Nobody is perfect and that's ok** – Literally nobody, it's time to believe it.
- **Never lose hope** – People are great. Life is great. Things work out.
- **There's always another way** – You might not be used to it. You might not like it, but it doesn't make it wrong.
- **Don't forget to enjoy the view** – Life zips by. Be sure to take it all in. Don't wish your time away.
- **Just keep swimming** – This is an important one. Life throws a lot of shit at us. It's important to keep going.

So many of us have forgotten these 5 things. So many, like Dory, have lost their way. Lost their way in a sea of envy, a sea of comparison, a sea of screens. I introduced you earlier to NEMO (Not Entirely Missing Out) and while this is definitely an important first step, may I now introduce DORY (Discovery of the Real You).

I urge you to let go. Literally, of your phone. But most importantly, let go of this idea that perfect exists. Expecting perfection does not lead to happiness. Replace perfection with progress and contentment. I urge you to look up from your phone and look around.

As actor Jonah Hill says, maybe the most convincing sign that someone is truly living their best life, is their lack of desire to show the world that they're living their best life.

I urge you to find DORY and embrace the person you discover. Not the 'you' on Instagram. The real you.

'Offline is the new luxury.'

—*Anon*

Quick task!

Grab a pen and in the space below list 5 ways in which your life would be better without a phone. Pay close attention to the things on your list.

_____

_____

_____

_____

_____

_____

_____

_____

_____

_____

_____

_____

_____

_____

_____

Screenage Kicks

I'm old enough to remember what it was like to have no smart phone. In fact, any mobile phone. And it was bliss. I didn't know that at the time but looking back I see it now.

I'm absolutely over the moon that SMART phones weren't around when I was a teenager. You might find that a weird concept.

I am genuinely delighted. I was distracted enough by everything else. I reckon if phones were added into the mix, I would have found everything way more difficult than I did. And the fear of having my every movement filmed by some of the dickheads I went to school with? Nah, no thanks!

At an event in a school, I was discussing this very topic with a crowd of 13-year-olds. I mentioned that I remember not having a mobile phone. The entire room burst out laughing. The following conversation ensued . . .

> **Girl**: 'But how did you speak to your friends?'
> **Gav**: 'You walked to their house. Or cycled.'
>
> *Laughter*
>
> **Girl**: [puzzled expression] 'What if they lived in the next town?'
>
> **Gav**: 'You walked to their house. Or you cycled.'
>
> *More laughter*
>
> **Girl**: 'What if they live too far for that?'
>
> **Gav**: 'You picked up the house phone.'

A moment's silence from the kids while they looked at each other

Girl: 'What's a "house phone"?'

Gav: 'You know. The phone you have at home that sits halfway up the stairs and no one uses but your parents still pay for it anyway?'

Laughter

Girl: 'But what if they lived in another country and it was too expensive to call?'

Gav: [starting to feel silly] 'You wrote a letter. And posted it.'

More laughter

Girl: 'What if you were out seeing friends and you weren't going to make it home at the time your mum said you needed to be home by?'

Gav: 'You found a phone box and reversed the charges. If your mum accepted the call, you were fine. If she didn't, you were in trouble.'

Silence

Gav: 'Reversing the charges? Anyone?'

Silence

Ask your parents. . . .

The young teens in the room proceeded to remind me yet again of the positives. You can download music, order takeaway dinners, watch films, book a taxi, you can basically order whatever you want these days. You can record your favourite TV shows, watch live action from the football field, watch the action from actual battlefields, turn your lights off, listen to any song you want, and you can even post pictures of yourself for absolutely no reason whatsoever other than to be validated by complete strangers who actually don't care about you.

We can do some cool stuff but there's a side to it all that we know isn't good. Yet many of us choose it. Every day for the last ten years I've contemplated chucking my phone away. I hate it. I hate everything about it.

Why? Coz I KEEP ON LOOKING AT IT! And 99% of the time what do I see?

Nothing. Nothing that matters. Nothing important. Nothing meaningful. Social media is the worst for this. I know this and you know this.

I looked at one of my accounts the other day and someone had posted the following . . .

'Can you believe some people?!'

That's it! Eh? Why would anyone feel the need to post this? What does it even mean? In turn, of course, the comments posted below went as follows . . .

>*'You alright hun?'*
>*'Call me?'*
>*'You keep smiling babe, know who your real friends are.'*

Yeah, because your real friends are most definitely your social media friends.

The worst part is the fact I spent 15 minutes reading and then thinking about this. Now, it takes less than 30 seconds to read it, so what was I doing? Staring. Staring at comments that made me angry and now I'M WRITING ABOUT IT IN MY NEW BOOK!

Compare and Despair

But we also have a responsibility to others. To the world. To be honest, yes, but to care. To be kind.

'In a world of algorithms, hashtags, and followers, know the true importance of human connection.'

—Anon

It's a tough one, as technology and the modern rules of life have solved many old problems, but as highlighted previously it's delivering new psychological challenges. We can now add to this social problems too. Mary Aiken, author of *The Cyber Effect*, tells us what we probably already know, that when we're online we can develop an impaired sense of judgement.

Dr Andy Cope refers to our online persona as the 'real-world equivalent of Harry Potter's invisibility cloak'. Once unseen you become imbued with magical powers, aka the 'online disinhibition effect' (ODE).

A TROLL
. . .

In other words, when they can't be seen, some find themselves a wee bit braver than normal and say or do things they perhaps wouldn't in 'real' life. Because in real life, you're a nice person, right?

You've seen it for yourself. The other side to being online, the dark side. And it ruins lives.

Firstly, there's the Me Brigade. I'm not talking about those of us who occasionally post a lovely picture of a family day trip. I'm referring to the narcissists. 'Oh look at me everyone, look at my new car, my new house, my new holiday, here's a picture of my face, me, me, me and while we're at it, here's my face again, LOOK AT MY FACE, QUACK!'

Then there's the bullies, the trolls. I cannot even begin to contemplate jumping on to something like Twitter and sending a nasty comment to someone I know, let alone a death threat to a complete stranger. WTAF? I just don't get it. We're allowed to not like something, we're allowed to disagree, we're even allowed to not like some*one*. But that's no excuse to be a dick. We can still show respect. We can still have empathy. We can still understand the difference between right and wrong.

Experts like Richard Layard tell us 'if you care more about other people relative to yourself, you are more likely to be happy.' There it is again, being kind to others makes us happier. So what if someone else has different political views to you. So what if they support a different football team. So what if they listen to BTS but you like the Foo's. IT'S NOT A REASON TO SEND THEM HORRIBLE SHIT ONLINE.

In the words of Dr Andy Cope, 'Empathy is the cornerstone of good relationships and good relationships are the cornerstone of happiness.'

I've already made it clear that I'm not going to tell you to stop using your phone. But if that's all you do then what's it doing to your real-life relationships? If all you do is sit in your room scrolling then that's not real-life human connection. It's scrolling.

Imagine how many miles we've scrolled with our thumbs. In a million years our thumbs will be massive. We'll be ruled by thumbs. 5 million years . . . we'll *be* thumbs.

Remember being 10, when we sat down on a Saturday night as a family to watch TV? Together? We'd laugh together, chat together, eat together, share together. Compare this to the modern Saturday night experience. We all sit down together to watch TV, on our phones, laptops and tablets. Several screens all on the go at the same time. We don't laugh at the same time anymore, we don't chat anymore, we don't share the moment anymore. You're probably in your room.

Ok, maybe it's not quite like that. It's not that we don't do those things anymore, but that we do them much less often. Ditto mealtimes. How many of you are guilty of sitting down at mealtimes and everyone is on their phone? Do you even notice what you're eating? Are you paying attention to each other? If you're with your family or out with friends, then why do you even need a phone?

More and more now we see parents with their children eating in restaurants and the kids get handed phones or tablets. It's so sad when you see mum and dad on their phones and the child sits staring into space with no one to talk to.

How many of us lie in bed at the end of a day, staring at our phones? How many of us wake up in the morning and the first thing we do is reach for the phone? It's like a drug. We need that hit in the morning.

I was chatting with some teenagers about this recently and one of them told me they spend at least an hour a day on Snapchat. Another told me he's at least an hour a day on TikTok. I told them I thought that was crazy and one gave me the following response. . . .

'But what would you do instead?'

Are you kidding me?

LIVE.

I'd live my life.

One hour a day, every day of the year is 365 hours a year. 365 hours a year is over 15 days a year. FIFTEEN DAYS A YEAR ON SNAPCHAT AND TIKTOK. Over 30 years that's 450 days which in itself is one year and 85 days. So basically 1 year and 3 months.

Let that sink in. If your phone is telling you that you spend an hour a day on any social media platform then you are giving away 15 days a year to scrolling. Just think, over a 30-year period you could be spending 1 year and 3 months on Snapchat or TikTok watching people dance.

And then there's Twitter and Instagram. And Facebook and everything else that goes with your phone.

I also chatted with some teenagers recently who told me they spend about 6 hours a day on social media.

6 hours.

That's 91 days a year. Over 30 years that's approximately 7.5 years.

SEVEN AND A HALF YEARS LOOKING AT YOUR PHONE.

Some people argue that your generation are the generation who rarely look up, who appear to prefer documenting their life rather than living it.

Some experts say the 'freedom tool' has become your captor.

Some say you're the generation trapped in a loop of 'phoney productivity'.

But many of you say, 'So what?' 'The entire world is on my phone, surely that's awesome?'

This is not some kind of teenage call to arms to stop using your phones, but we all have a responsibility to ourselves. To make sure we are giving ourselves the best chance to be healthy and happy. To simply be.

No Expense Spared

Economics has a phrase, 'opportunity cost', a wonderful way of getting you to think about the price of the next best alternative. You, for example: if you spend 8 hours a day scrolling, that's 8 hours that you could have been doing something else.

'Being famous on Instagram is basically the same thing as being rich in Monopoly.'

—Anon

Everything you ever do has an opportunity cost. Time has an opportunity cost. Reading this book has an opportunity cost. You could have been studying or helping your mum make the dinner. But it works the other way too. For all the time you spend studying, you could be making TikTok's, scrolling, collecting 'likes'.

Nick Carr warns that online activity such as email and social media cause people to become addicted to 'mindlessly pressing levers in the hope of receiving a pellet of social or intellectual nourishment'.

But it's bigger than that.

The problem with all the hours spent on your phone is that these are hours that you are not going to get back. They cost time. These hours have an opportunity cost. You are not playing with your wee brother, chatting with your family at the dinner table, visiting your old granny who might not be around much longer, kicking a ball about at the park or forming a band with your best weirdos.

I use my phone a lot for business, I do the social media thing, I'm not perfect and I don't always get it right. But a few years ago, when someone told me that 'it can cost your life', I shat it.

I realised I was hooked.

Everywhere, everyone is engaged, always. Our heads are busy places, *many* of us are so switched on we struggle to stop, to relax, to switch off, to be. And now many of us pay for silence. We pay for mindfulness apps, courses and so on. Many of us have lost the ability to stop, to relax, to have peace of mind.

The urge to reach for the phone is there 24 hours a day for some. Many of the teenagers I work with report waking up through the night 'needing' to reach for the phone. It used to be that the older we got the more likely we'd wake up through the night needing a pee.

Families watching a movie together, but Mum's checking her Instagram. Couples out for a meal, just the two of them together, sitting across from each other, in love, romantically looking into their phone screens. Friends all hanging out, staring at their phones. Dad playing with his kids while scrolling and not actually paying any attention to what his children are doing.

For anyone reading this feeling their blood boil because you do this and you're feeling victimised, unfairly singled out, I assure you my blood is boiling too as I've done all of the above. And I know it's wrong, just like you do. And that's why you're angry right now. Because you're a bit shit sometimes at putting your phone down and being present.

In his TED-Ed Blog 'Why we owe it to ourselves to spend quiet time alone every day', Alan Lightman claims that by not giving ourselves the minutes – or hours – free of devices and distractions, we risk losing our ability to know who we are and what's important to us.

He's spot on. It's already happening. We have teenagers and adults alike, more interested in collecting likes and being validated by complete strangers than going to bed. We have people of all ages unable to put their phones down when their family are telling them their daily news.

When COVID hit the world and everything stopped, many of us rediscovered time. Time for reflection. Time for contemplation. Time for privacy. Time for creativity. Time for each other.

I rediscovered that sitting for twenty minutes without any external stimulation is a joy.

I refer back to those who spend an hour a day on TikTok. What benefit could there be to spending that hour differently? An hour a day exercising, practising mindfulness or simply doing nothing, reflecting, being.

Here's my top 10 tips to spending less time on your phone. And trust me, this stuff makes a difference.

1. Download one of the many apps that tell you how long you're spending on your phone. Trust me, you'll shit yourself so much you'll cut down.
2. Kill the notifications. All of them.
3. Be ruthless with your apps – pick the ones you think you spend too much time on and delete them from your phone. You can still use them on your laptop, etc.
4. Keep your phone in another room. Studies have shown that people who *don't* charge their phone in their bedroom are happier!
5. Choose an ideal time of day to switch your phone off. And then stick to it.
6. Do other stuff. Seriously, pick up a guitar, buy a notebook and start writing, go running.
7. Instead of thinking about 'spending less time on your phone,' think about 'spending more time on your life'.
8. Keep your phone away from the dinner table. Try talking to your family.
9. Ask yourself regularly, how strong do I want my thumbs to be? In other words, how much of my life do I want to spend scrolling?
10. Have a weekend away. From your phone. Off-grid. Trust me, you will love it so much, you'll do it more.

I know I said this was a top 10, but like life, we can always turn things up to 11. So here it is, the one that is just so easy and yet we always forget. . .

11. Everyone doesn't need access to you. If there is *anyone* at all that makes you feel shit, anyone at all, even family members! Hide, block or remove them from your timelines. You are allowed to do this.

If I can bring this full circle before I move on from phones . . .

Freddie Mercury sang 'Is this the real life? Is this just fantasy? Caught in a landslide, no escape from reality. Open your eyes, look up to the skies and see. . . .'

Real life can suck, and we all need some fantasy, some sense of escapism. We can all at times feel stuck and our phones provide us the gateway we often need to escape our busy lives.

But when we truly open our eyes to the real world and do all we need to do to discover the real you, it's incredible what we begin to notice.

The point of this section isn't to get you off the internet, or even off social media. It's simply about unhooking your brain from routines it has adopted around that device in your hand, and hooking it to better things.

This is about Finding NEMO, or perhaps more importantly, Finding DORY.

This is about hooking into yourself and being happy in your actual real life!

PS – You searched up the goat eating a Dorito, didn't you?

" **I dare you, in a world that entices us to browse through the lives of others to help us better determine how we feel about ourselves and to in turn feel the need to be constantly visible, for visibility these days seems to somehow equate to success - do not be afraid to disappear from it for a while, and see what comes to you in the silence.** "

—Michaela Cole

CHAPTER 6

Putting
the Trolley Away

Every Lidl Helps

Every now and then something brilliant appears online that stops you in your tracks.

A Public Policy Survey in 2016 found that nearly 12 million people believe that an elite class of space-travelling lizards rule the earth. Among these lizards is apparently Justin Bieber, who was reported earlier this year to have shape-shifted mid-concert into a giant reptile with 'big scaly claws' and 'a black stripe down its middle.'

Read that again.

12 million people believed this. 12 MILLION PEOPLE!

That's the power of the internet.

Starting July 2014, we started seeing videos of people pouring a bucket of ice over themselves, popping up all over our social media. The Ice Bucket Challenge, sometimes more appropriately called the ALS Ice Bucket Challenge, blew up all across the world and became a trending campaign to promote awareness on amyotrophic lateral sclerosis (ALS), also known as motor neuron disease (MND). The internet trend ended up raising over $115 million for the ALS Association, which helped the research team make a significant discovery.

Again, the power of the internet.

In 2021, as the world remained locked down during the pandemic, a simple idea was posted anonymously online, essentially suggesting a unique way to determine whether you were a good person or not. And like many things on the internet, it blew up big time and shocked many into reconsidering their behaviours.

'No one ever made a difference by being like everyone else.'

—P.T. Barnum

This is the Shopping Trolley Theory.

Going to the supermarket is not uncommon, we've all done it. At times we might just pop in to grab a couple of items but occasionally life requires a big shop. You may call it the weekly shopping, but in my house, it's the big shop. And the big shop requires a trolley.

Now, shopping trolleys are pretty much the same the world over. We've all seen one, we've all pushed one, we've all filled one, we've all sat in one and we've all lay across the top of one while our friends or siblings push us through supermarket aisles at great speeds. We've all emptied the contents of our trolley onto the checkout for it to be scanned and we've all refilled it, once bagged and paid for.

I understand this doesn't sound like the making of a potentially life-changing theory but stick with me, for this is about to change.

You head for the doors and you leave with a trolley full of supermarket treasures. You head for the car. It's further away than you remember. Mum, Dad, whoever it is you are with unlocks the car and you open the boot. All the shopping bags are hoisted out of the trolley and into the car.

You know what happens next, don't you? Someone needs to return the trolley. The job in hand often naturally defaults to the non-driver of the group. And as the teenager, you're expected to deliver.

You can either return the trolley to the actual supermarket itself, or you can return it to one of the many trolley bays scattered across the car park, designed to make life easier for those of us in a hurry.

It's just that sometimes you find yourself parked a fair distance from said supermarket or said trolley bay.

You are faced with dilemma. To return? Or, not to return? That is the question.

And this dear reader, is where it gets interesting. . . .

To return the shopping trolley is an easy, convenient task and one that we all recognise as the correct, appropriate thing to do.

To return the shopping trolley is, in its simplest form, the right thing to do. And plus, let's not forget you'll get your pound coin back.

There are very few reasons to *not* return the trolley. Dire emergencies, young kids in the car or perhaps you are physically unable to, I'll give you all of these but aside from that, returning the trolley is the right thing to do. It doesn't matter that it's someone else's job to put the trollies away.

But, it's not illegal to not return it. It's not illegal to abandon your trolley in the middle of the car park or on a pavement nearby. No one will punish you. You won't receive a fine, you definitely won't be going to jail and it's not going to kill you.

Therefore, the shopping trolley presents itself as the perfect example of whether a person will do what is right without being forced to do it.

You gain nothing from returning the shopping trolley. In other words, you must return the shopping trolley out of the goodness of your own heart. You must return the shopping trolley because it is the right thing to do. Because it is correct.

The theory claims that the humble shopping trolley is what determines whether a person is a good or bad member of society. Now, some might feel that's pushing it a little; in your mind the whole thing might seem far-fetched or perhaps overly simplistic.

But it stopped me in my tracks.

The shopping trolley theory for me is representative of so many moments in life where we find ourselves faced with a very simple decision of doing the right thing or not.

Picking up litter. Picking up dog poo. Tidying your room. Studying for an exam. Preparing for a job interview. Helping your parents. Babysitting your younger siblings. Saying 'thank you'. I could keep going!

Quite often, doing the right thing requires a bit more energy, a bit more effort. But here's the thing, we feel better for doing it. There's always the easy route.

This whole thing is about being in a moment and making a decision. The right decision.

So, before we move on. In life we are faced with a continuous, daily decision-making dilemma. If you find yourself presented with one of these moments and you know what the right thing is to do but there is an easier quicker way, no matter how much more effort is involved, how much more time it will take, just think to yourself, 'Put the trolley away'.

Not Enough Meat on the Bones

One of the biggest 'Trolley Moments' for me all through my teens was homework and studying for exams.

I reckon I'm the world's best procrastinator. A mighty declaration to make in a world full of procrastinators. I'm not proud of it but I am brilliant at it. Ninja level good. 5th dan procrastinator.

I'm making the assumption here that you know what procrastination means? Apologies if I'm about to patronise you. Patronise, that's when I tell you something you already know. . . . That right there is a very clever joke. Well, in my mind anyway. I'll move on.

pro-cras-ti-na-tion
noun
the action of delaying or postponing something: *your first tip is to avoid procrastination*.

So, the question was always 'To study . . . or not to study?' Put the trolley away or just leave it for someone else to worry about. After all, just what could go wrong? I'll come back to this question shortly. . . .

In other words, I am a self-confessed world champion puterofferer!

Puterofferer
Poo-ter-off-er-er
noun
someone who can't stop looking out the window imagining the seagulls are in fact having a disco, thumbing at Instagram and WhatsApping mates, instead of doing the thing that they're meant to be doing, that they know is proper important.

The ability to put things off or certainly leave them to the last minute comes very naturally to me. I have, however, become better with age at combatting this. Big grown-up deadlines with financial implications definitely – at times – provide the boot up the backside often required.

But as a teenager, my ability to leave things such as studying and homework to the last minute was second to none. I didn't enjoy it. I knew it was important and the right thing to do but my head was often up my backside. It was boring.

The result was often a half-assed attempt to produce something passable in record time. Every single parents' night my teachers told my parents the same thing, 'he's capable, there's just not enough meat on the bones.'

Of course, as the essays got longer and the content more complicated, the greater the level of focus required. It was here my ability to put things off reached new heights. I could sit for hours staring at a wall. Bear in mind this was pre–social media days. No mobile phones. No YouTube. I reckon throughout my school career I literally spent months dreaming up new wallpaper patterns.

I can recall having an assignment due in on a Monday morning. I started it on the Sunday evening at 7 pm. I had been given the work three weeks prior. At 7 pm, I sat down, picked up a pen and by 10 pm I had successfully made an origami swan. I worked entirely from memory after an art lesson 9 years previously and genuinely felt a sense of achievement. It was a beautiful swan, but no assignment completed, yet.

The assignment was on Apartheid in South Africa. Not origami. Or swans.

I still got the assignment handed in. And passed. But only just.

'"I'm bored" is a useless thing to say. I mean, you live in a great, big, vast world that you've seen none percent of. Even the inside of your own mind is endless; it goes on forever, inwardly, do you understand? The fact that you're alive is amazing, so you don't get to say "I'm bored".'

—Louis C.K.

I love the way author and speaker Tim Urban writes about the difference between the brain of a procrastinator and that of a non-procrastinator.

He challenges us to imagine both brains having a wee person in them, standing at a ships wheel, steering us through life. Tim calls this wee person our 'Rational Decision-Maker'. We all have one.

In both brains, the 'Rational Decision-Maker' wants the same thing, and both believe they are able to make good decisions and take appropriate action in life. Again, we all have one.

According to Tim, the main different between a puterofferer and non-puterofferer is that the brain of a puterofferer is also inhabited by a small primate that he calls the 'Instant Gratification Monkey'.

It was only after reading Tim's work that I was able to finally understand just what was going on in my head. I was 30 years old when I had this breakthrough. 30. . . .

In my mind, all these years I've had, in Tim's words, an 'Instant Gratification Monkey' living alongside my 'Rational Decision-Maker'.

I have a feeling that right now your thinking is something along the lines of . . . 'What the hell is an Instant Gratification Monkey?'

Let me explain. . . .

Basically, the 'Rational Decision-Maker' is the sensible voice in your head that says things like 'Now is the perfect time to get some work done. I'm going to sit at my desk and smash my studying. Put the trolley away.'

The 'Instant Gratification Monkey' is the other voice in your head that says, 'Oooh look, a squirrel! I'm going to call it Barry and watch him for an hour.'

Here's the problem, no one's 'Rational Decision-Maker' knows the first thing about how to own a monkey. Unfortunately, it wasn't a part of the training, and 'Rational Decision-Maker' is left completely helpless as the monkey makes it impossible for him/her to do their job.

Here's the even bigger problem, the 'Rational Decision-Maker' doesn't understand the 'Instant Gratification Monkey' and the 'Instant Gratification Monkey' doesn't understand the 'Rational Decision-maker'.

The following is a genuine conversation I had literally yesterday in my head. You can see it clearly demonstrates the work of both my 'Rational Decision-Maker' and my 'Instant Gratification Monkey'.

I'm going to go on a run.

But running isn't much fun.

It's really good for me, always feel good afterwards.

It hurts a bit. Might jump on YouTube.

I'll do 5k and then have a big healthy bowl of porridge.

I'll skip my run today, oh look, chips. YouTube.

I skipped my run and ate chips. And I ate them in a sandwich while going down a massive YouTube wormhole. Don't get me wrong, it was delicious and thoroughly entertaining, but the monkey won. The trolley was well and truly left in the middle of the car park.

The monkey thinks *only* about the present, ignores any lessons learned from previous slip-ups, doesn't even begin to think about the future and what implications this may have. Basically, he/she is all about making sure that right now is lovely and fun and easy.

For monkeys it's easy, eat when you're hungry, sleep when you're tired, don't do anything too difficult and you'll be a pretty successful monkey.

The problem for you and I is that we are human and we live in the human world. I'm not sure about you but I'm happy to admit that I'm rubbish at fighting monkeys, and the more he's in control, the worse I feel.

It's in this moment we procrastinators spend a lot of time in what Tim Urban calls the 'Dark Playground'. He describes it as 'a place where leisure activities happen at times when leisure activities are not supposed to be happening'.

In other words, the fun we're having isn't actually fun because deep down you know you've not earned it and that underlying feeling of guilt, anxiety and dread is slowly but surely building. The thing that you're meant to be doing, that really needs to be done, will still be there needing to be done when you've finished pouring through TikTok for an hour.

It's that bloody opportunity cost thing again from earlier!

'The secret of getting ahead is getting started.'

—*Sally Berger*

So just how does a procrastinator ever manage to get things done?

For me the answer is pure fear. Tim Urban calls it the 'Panic Monster'. It suddenly wakes up when a deadline is fast approaching or there's any chance whatsoever of being left looking like a fool in public or anything that has any kind of scary consequences.

The Instant Gratification Monkey is terrified of the Panic Monster. Tim nails it when he asks, 'How else could you explain the same person who can't write a paper's introductory sentence over a two-week span suddenly having the ability to stay up all night, fighting exhaustion, and write eight pages?'

I know from experience this is no way to live. It's awful and you end up selling yourself short, focussing on all things needing to be done rather than the thing you want to be doing.

So, let's talk about something that plays a huge part in our young adult lives, something that can play on your mind, eat away at us, forming the basis of so many conversations and that is often the root cause of so much stress and heartache.

Nope, not boyfriends and girlfriends . . . or sex.

Exams.

As much as I can't stand them, I can't write a book for teenagers and not mention them.

For reference, I'm one of those types who believe there's too many tests in schools and the whole exam process is in dire need of a complete overhaul. Anyway, whilst I'm absolutely not an authority voice when it comes to exams, I am more than happy to state, I'm not a fan.

But they exist. And just as I did in my teens, it is almost guaranteed that you will – and may have already – be sitting some exams over the coming months or years. These could be smaller, less important exams that still feel quite scary at the time, or the bigger, more important exams that can determine your next steps in life.

Now, I say 'determine your next steps' with some caution. Yes, they can determine if you go to university, college, etc., or even *which* university or college but . . . and it is a big BUT . . . your exams do not determine who you are or the rest of your life. They do not define you.

I have no issues telling you here that as a business owner and an employer of several people, at no point do I take anyone's school exam results into consideration when recruiting for any role in my organisation. I'm looking for great humans with real character.

I do, however, want to know that when I go for an operation in hospital that my surgeon has passed all the necessary exams and are fully qualified up to their eyeballs to be removing my appendix and not just a good person!

While your school qualifications *can* impact upon your life in the moment, in time only *you* and *your* attitude to life will steer you through to where you want to be. Remember, you are what you think.

Your exams are not the be all and end all. Yes, get stuck in and give it your all. Try your best, always. But if you fail, make sure you fail gloriously. By that, I mean fail knowing you couldn't have done any more. Take that failure and pull all the learning from it that you can. Talk it out loud with your teachers, parents and friends and remain proud.

For anyone reading this who has recently received their exam results or will in time receive theirs, keep the following in mind . . .

First up, let's just give a nod to those who absolutely smash it out of the park, always. You know the ones. Those of you who get the most phenomenal grades you could ever imagine and find themselves set to go live your dream at the dream university or whatever you've chosen. You can chill, party, relax, whatever, you're sorted for now, well done, I salute you!

Even those who just scraped by, by the skin of your teeth. You did it, you're there, magic, I salute you also!

 And actually, a wee note also to those of you who completely and utterly fluke it. Those who do NOTHING and yet somehow, *somehow*, I've no idea how you people do this, but somehow you managed to get yourself some excellent grades! I take my hat off to you as well, well done, saluting yet again.

But I want to acknowledge those of you who don't quite end up with the results you had hoped for. Those who maybe fail way more than anticipated, perhaps flunked the whole thing entirely or maybe only just miss out by the tiniest wee amount on the grades or the credits that you needed. Either way, a fail's a fail. And failure sucks.

I feel your pain. You'll probably end up feeling really pissed off. You'll probably get those pangs of guilt, frustration, anger, embarrassment, all made worse by people saying things like 'put it in perspective'.

I get the sentiment behind advice like this but it's the worst advice to hear when you're feeling the way you're feeling in this moment.

'Don't let other people decide who you are.'

—Anon

Do you know what's going to happen if you ever find yourself in this situation?

Whatever you want.

That's it.

Whatever you want can still happen.

Again, your exams do not define you. They are not the be all and end all.

They *can* be really important, but they don't *have* to be!

What I recommend you do, is take a day. 24 hours. And lie in your bed and shove ice cream into your face. That will help. How do I know? Because that's what I did. Actually, I reckon I gave myself 2–3 days of feeling sorry for myself. I cried a good bit too.

And then I went and did something about it.

Dear Parents,

I see your flaws.

I'm learning from ~~you~~.

Your Teenager

x

Results Day

16 years old and I hadn't slept a wink all night. I knew I hadn't done well. How? Simple, I just hadn't done enough and that's what kept me awake all night. I knew what was coming, I could just feel it.

I got out my bed early hoping I'd perhaps catch the postie early. Keep in mind this was before the days of exam results coming in via text message or email. I was awaiting my brown envelope with my laminated certificate inside. It was this very laminated certificate that was to drop an almighty bomb right on my teenage existence.

I stood at the window, waiting.

I had sat exams before. 12 months before to be exact. I had done reasonably well, for me. I'm not the most academic human on the planet but I tried hard.

This time, however, everything was tougher, everything felt bigger. The commitment, the work, the hours, the pressure, the stress, the prize. All of it seemed so much more than before. Teachers talking about it, friends talking about it, parents talking about it, the radio talking about it, TV talking about it. University places were at stake. The pressure to go to uni was huge. I didn't even know if I wanted to go.

It was all too much. I'd spent the year worrying to such an extent that when it came to doing the actual work, I just couldn't. It wasn't laziness, it was all sorts of worry.

With no sign of my results, I grabbed my jacket and left. I figured I might be able to speed the inevitable up by heading out and finding the postie myself. I lived in a very small town, and I knew there was a good chance of finding him. And I did.

Two streets away, there he was. His post bag laden down with many a teen's apparent future life stuffed inside a brown envelope.

I was out of breath from running.

'Morning, do you have my results?' I puffed.

'As you can see, I have *all* the results!' he replied, pointing to his postbag.

'Cool, I live at number. . . .'

'You could say I'm the guardian of your future,' he interrupted.

'Eh, ok, can I please have results?'

'Ooh, is someone a little stressed this morning, worried about what news this postman will deliver today?'

At this point I would happily have fought him for them.

'Dude, can I please have my results?'

I gave him my address, he gave me my envelope and as I ran off he shouted . . .

'I hope you've done better than you think?'

I appreciated his words, I like to think he could see it in my eyes that I was worried. I ran back to my house.

I snuck into the living room. At the time I didn't think my parents were even awake, but I know now they saw me leave the house.

I sat staring at my envelope like Charlie Bucket staring at his Wonka chocolate bar. Would opening this change my life forever?

I opened it carefully and very slowly pulled my certificate out.

Now, before I share my results with you, let me firstly explain how things used to work in Scotland.

When I sat exams at school, an A was a pass, a B was a pass and a C was a pass. Naturally A's were worth more, then B's, then C's. But all still considered a pass.

Here's where it got confusing; a D, whilst listed on your certificate, was considered a fail. It counted for nothing. Anything less than a D, didn't even appear on the certificate. They were officially known as 'No Awards'. Or, as we called them, 'Nae mentions'.

I slowly pulled the certificate from the envelope. I was waiting for the results to appear. Slowly but surely the certificate was leaving the envelope, still nothing appearing. This was very much looking like a blank certificate.

Surely not? Surely no one ever, *ever*, has been sent a blank certificate? That would mean of the four exams I sat, *all* were 'No Awards'. Four 'Nae Mentions'. Four fails. Everything failed.

Everything.

From in the kitchen, I heard a cork popping. My mum and dad had been hoping for big things, they believed in me and now was a time to celebrate. I have an older brother who had done great 2 years before. Another added pressure.

Except they didn't know yet that I had a blank certificate. No one in my family had ever had a blank certificate. I was the first proper failure in my family.

My life flashed before me.

I could hear Mum and Dad coming through, the glasses clinking on the tray . . .

They knocked the door and Mum stuck her head round the door.

'Well?' she asked.

'Well . . .' I replied.

'How'd you do?' she asked.

'Erm, I didn't', I replied.

Mum's face seemed to change very quickly. Went very serious.

'You didn't what?' she asked.

'I didn't do . . .' I replied.

'You didn't do what, Gavin?' she asked with a very different tone.

To which all I could say was, 'Anything'.

'When life shuts a door, open it again. It's a door. That's how they work.'

—*Anon*

I could hear my dad taking the champagne back to the kitchen. We weren't really a champagne kind of family, but this had meant so much to them. Possibly more than it had to me. It's not that I didn't care about my future, I really did and still do. It's just exams weren't and still aren't my thing.

Mum sat down on the sofa opposite me and said nothing. She had that look of 'I'm not angry, I'm just disappointed'. You'll know that look, the one that hurts the most.

I just sat.

And sat.

And sat some more.

I'm not sure how long I actually sat for, but it was a while.

All I could think about was what I wanted to achieve in life. Why did I have to sit all these exams in order to get me there? Why didn't I just put the work in? Why can't I be super clever like others? What am I actually good at?

The questions just kept coming and, in this moment, I didn't really have any answers. All I knew, was that right now, I didn't like the way I was feeling very much.

My parents came into the room again and started talking. For the first time ever I didn't talk back, I didn't get defensive, I just listened.

Turns out my parents had some cool stuff to say. Turns out they had been through some crazy things in life I had never heard about. They shared a tonne of stuff they had learned through their lives. I saw a different side to them. I just kept listening.

Listening to my mum and dad that day, I realised something had to change. And it needed to start with me. It needed to start in my head.

It was time to start putting the trolley away!

Dear Parents,

I'm going to make tomes of mistakes.
All of which you probably made too.
Remember that when you talk to me about it after.

Your Teenager

x

Unpopular Opinion

Your parents are cooler than you. And your teachers are too.

I know you desperately don't want to believe me, but they are. You might want to argue that it depends on the definition of cool because at your age being 'cool' is usually associated with popularity. But some of you will already be realising that it's so much more than this.

'It's a funny thing about mothers and fathers. Even when their own child is the most disgusting little blister you could ever imagine, they still think that he or she is wonderful.'

—Matilda *by Roald Dahl*

Here's 10 reasons I'm right.

1. **They've done more awesome things than you.**
   Many of which you don't know about and some of which you just wouldn't believe. Why do you not know about them? Probably because now is not the time or some of it just won't be for sharing. The more you move through your teens, the more you start to learn about them, the more they begin to tell you. The odd, casual conversation here and there, there's stuff that will make you sit up and notice. There will be things that blow your mind. That's cool.

2. **They give to you continuously.**
   They spend their life trying to create, offer and give new experiences to you. That's what parents and teachers do and they look for no thanks, ever, and that's cool.

3. **They do nice things just because they can.**
   They run after you constantly. Doesn't matter what mood you are in, where your head's at or how you're treating them, they're like a gift that just keeps on giving. Don't get me wrong, most of us are nice, especially when we're meant to be. Parents and teachers are nice even when no one would expect them to be. Not because they have to. Just because they can, and that's cool.

4. **They big you up.**
   Parents and teachers constantly try to prove to you that you're amazing, that you can tackle anything head on and make a great life for yourself and that's cool.

5. **They find happiness in your happiness.**
   For centuries, the greatest thinkers have told us the same thing; happiness is found in helping others. That's what parents and teachers do, it's their job. All they want is to see you happy. Helping can be tiring but they're willing to exhaust themselves for you, and that's cool.

6. **They stick to their principles.**
   Our parents and teachers often believe in us more than we do. Yours will have a strong belief in you and make choices in their daily lives to do the right thing by you, even if that means going against the grain, and that's cool.

7. **They can forgive and forget.**
   We say and do some awful things to our parents and teachers in our teens. And just so you know, it hurts real bad. But they take it, they know deep down you don't mean it and they move on with what's important, and that's cool.

8. **They're almost always right.**
   Nobody is always right. Even the best can get it wrong at times but contrary to popular opinion, parents and teachers know a lot more than you, have experienced more than you, have failed

more than you, have succeeded more than you and with that in mind are almost always right, and that's cool.

9. **They don't think they're cool.**

   Social media makes it's easy nowadays to take care of your own hype. You can blow your own trumpet, bask in the glow of your wit and accomplishments. With a little time and effort you can seem larger than life. Chances are your parents and teachers don't do that. They just focus on working hard to give you the best in life that they can. This is why they're humble, why they ask questions and still to this day seek advice from others, and that's cool.

10. **They don't focus on highlighting how far *they've* come.**

    They focus on highlighting how far *you've* come! Always encouraging, always lifting, always reassuring. And then they invest their own time, energy and effort to help you go even further.

    Cool, huh?

    And guess what?

    There's a number 11 . . .

11. **They've partied harder than you.**

    Like, way harder. Trust me, they've seen and done it all. I don't care if that makes you cringe, I don't care if it makes you want to projectile vomit all over your room. It's true.

    I couldn't believe the stuff my parents came out with over time as they recounted tales from their younger days. At times I was so mortified, I nearly had to leave the room. Some of it I can't repeat here but I began to realise just how cool my parents were.

    I can't wait to tell my kids about my trips to Ibiza or my time doing stand up all over the world.

Read the list again. And read it properly. If you think being cool still means having the most 'likes' or the most 'followers' on TikTok then I obviously need to try harder.

But if you really want to know what cool is, then there's one more.

Number 12.

Number 12 is rarely spoken of. It's almost mythical.

And it's this . . .

12. **You grandparents have partied harder than your parents.**
It's your grandparents you need to speak to.  Trust me, they will have the most unbelievable stories about growing up and the things they got up to. They really have seen and done it all. ALL OF IT!

Let that sink in.

Now there's an image for you. . . .

> "The secret of the
> Muppets is they're not
> very good at what they do.
> Kermit is not a great host,
> Fozzie is not a good comedian,
> Miss Piggy is not a great singer...
> Like, none of them are
> actually good at it,
> but they love it!
> And they're like a family, and
> they like putting on the show,
> And they have joy.
> And because they have
> joy, it doesn't matter that
> they're not good at it.
> And that's what we should
> all be, Muppets!"

—*Brett Goldstein*

CHAPTER 7

Awkward!

Farts are funny. You know it and dads know it. Mums not so much. Well, some mums do. Probably something to do with the fact that lady pumps smell worse than man pumps. (This is scientifically true. No seriously, it is.)

You could argue that humans are obsessed with farts. Doing them, hearing them, blaming others for them and making the noise, real or not. Of all the bodily functions, this one is definitely the favourite.

Legendary comedian Billy Connolly once said that farts are just your bum cheeks clapping!

Did you know farts even have their own National Day on January 7th?

Guess what January 6th is? National Bean Day! Fact! Think about it. . . .

We love them so much we give them names. Here's some of my favourites. Air biscuit, Benchwarmer, Bottom Yodel,

Butt Sneeze, Mouse on a Motorcycle, Triple Thunder Flutter, Bum Clap and Free Jacuzzi.

I love farts. And I know you do too. My daughter is 9 and she can fart pretty much on demand. Such a skill! She farts a lot more than most.

Did you know that humans fart – on average – 14 times per day? How awesome is that? It works out about half a litre of farts per day.

Let's just say that once again . . . half a litre of farts per day. Another great name for a band, Half a Litre of Farts.

So, let's imagine there's 25 other teenagers in your class. Some classes will have more and some less, but we'll go with 25. You spend 6 hours a day in school. That's 25% of your day in school therefore you pump 25% of your farts at school.

25% of your farts is 3.5 farts. You do – on average – 3.5 farts in class per day.

25 teens doing 3.5 farts is 87.5 farts per day, per class. That's 6.25 litres of fart in your class, every day, that you basically swim in.

That's more than 24 cups of cheek squeak. Over 1.5 gallons of great brown cloud. 384 tablespoons of thunder from down under.

Around 1.15 million farts happen every second on earth. All the humans that have ever lived have released approximately 17 quadrillion farts, ever, and counting.

Did you know farts are also really fast? They've actually been clocked in at 3.05 meters per second, which is roughly

7 miles per hour. That's faster than your standard hoverboard, which are also, coincidentally, flammable.

Sometimes we think farts are disgusting because they stink of egg, but farting is just something a healthy human body does.

So basically, farts are completely natural, we need them, they're all around us, sometimes they take us by surprise, occasionally we like them, sometimes we really don't. They're better out than in. Some we can control and others we can't, *but* everyone produces them! And we must always remember, farting isn't gross.

Guess what?

Neither is having feelings. Feelings are completely natural, we need them, they're all around us, sometimes they take us by surprise, occasionally we like them, sometimes we really don't. They're better out than in. Some we can control and others we can't *but* everyone produces them! And we must always remember, having feelings isn't gross.

IT'S JUST SOMETHING A HEALTHY HUMAN BODY DOES.

Ok, so I confess, I could've just started this section talking about emotions, but I wanted to prove it's actually easier sometimes to talk about farting than it is our emotions and feelings. For some reason farts can be embarrassing but talking about our emotions and how we feel is – for some – next level.

The thing is, we feel more than we fart! Unless you're my daughter.

Emotions rule so much of our lives and yet it's almost impossible to describe the full range and experience of human emotions. It can be really hard to talk about how we are feeling. Proper experts will tell you that there are 27 unique emotions. I wonder how many you can name? I bet you can name 27 different types of fart much quicker!

It's normal to feel, yet practically impossible for some of us to talk about. Try and think of reasons you shouldn't talk about your feelings? There are none. Yeah. That's right. There is not a single reason on earth for why you should not talk about your feelings.

'Don't forget to drink water and get some sun. You're basically a houseplant with more complicated emotions.'

—Anon

Although, if you're anything like I was at your age, you'll definitely find it easier to talk about good feelings and emotions rather than the bad ones. Unless its romantic feelings. Even the words 'romantic feelings' makes me want to throw up.

Here's a crazy fact for you, talking about feelings is actually really good for you, especially the bad ones. That's a tough thing to do at times as we can be reluctant to open up. Learning to talk about both positive *and* negative emotions helps us to become better at sharing and helping others. It leads to better mental health. It can help us learn to deal with stress better. I know it's not always easy but with practice it does get easier.

Some teenagers know more about McDonalds than they do about their own feelings.

Sometimes it can feel really awkward sharing how you're feeling. It's also really awkward sometimes sharing a fart too . . . yet both are entirely natural and normal.

My dad once told me, 'If you can fart in front of someone and they don't judge you for it then you know they're someone special.' Still makes me laugh to this day.

It's all about trusting those around us.

Just like farts, emotions are often better out than in. Although, that being said, occasionally you do need to pick your moment. Oh, and if you hold a fart or your emotions in for too long and bottle them up, well, that starts to hurt and it's no longer good for you.

(Note: don't literally bottle your farts up, that's actually disgusting.)

One of the best ways to practice is to take any negative feelings and try turning them into positive ones. Next time you're asked/told to tidy your room, instead of feeling annoyed because you can't be bothered and it takes too long, turn it around in your head. Shift your thinking and tell yourself, 'If I just get this done now, I'll be able to enjoy it more and I'll feel better not being in a mess.'

Done.

It's really important at your age that you make the time to talk about how you're feeling, but actually humans of all ages need practice too.

Have you ever noticed that every single day after school, your parents *always* ask you how your day was? They then *always* ask what you've been up to, to which you usually reply 'Can't remember' or 'not much'. Right?

When was the last time you asked them?

Try to get into the habit of asking your parents/carers about *their* day. I dare you. Get them to tell you what happened at work and how it made them feel. Then, help them to turn any negative thoughts into positive ones. Seriously, try it. And do it every day for the next 7 days. You start the conversation with 'How was your day?' They'll be gobsmacked. And when they ask how yours was, tell them. Tell them your day was 'Amazing'. Look at their face. Then tell them what made it amazing. Be warned though, it's around about here they might collapse in shock and you might need to call an ambulance!

Dear Parents,
Don't be offended when I don't
tell you things.
Trust me that there is a reason.
It doesn't mean I don't
love you. ♡

Kind regards,
    Your Teenager
              xxx

Growing Pains

'Never be the reason why someone feels like shit. Be the reason they feel awake, elevated, empowered, and magical. That's it.'

—Anon

Speaking of farts, life is full of assholes. You'll meet them at every twist and turn. You'll hang out with them, you'll work for them, you'll vote for them and you'll see them on TV. But that doesn't mean you have to be one. If I was ever speaking out of turn or acting up in anyway, my dad used to say 'Gav, the world doesn't need another asshole.' That was his way of telling me I was being an asshole.

Every now and then one comes along and causes trouble. We all meet them at some point. And they bring out all sorts of feelings and emotions.

I was on day two hundred and something of being 17. I was over half way through my last year of high school and still my parents were telling me this year will be the best yet.

It hadn't been my best year, possibly the worst. I was hoping to finish school on a high but it felt like I was riding the year out on a massive low. I was still feeling the impact from having failed all my exams the year before. The pressure and stress of 'What's next?' and 'What if?' was building momentum, it formed the basis of every single conversation I was having, and I could feel it in every inch of my body.

Add to the mix all the usual teen pressures and it was all becoming a bit much. And things were about to get worse.

I had had some cool experiences in my time at school, got to do some cool things and meet some cool people. But none of this matters when someone decides they're going to ruin your life.

That's what bullies do. They don't bully by accident. They don't accidentally turn all your mates against you one by one. They don't accidently strip you of what little confidence you had.

Nah, they know exactly what they're doing. They decide. They choose their words very carefully and they have no idea of the sleepless nights those words then bring.

'You will always be too much of something for someone: too big, too loud, too soft, too edgy. If you round out your edges, you lose your edge. Apologize for mistakes. Apologize for unintentionally hurting someone – profusely. But don't apologize for being who you are.'

—*Danielle LaPorte*

No one really truly teaches us how to deal with bullies. We're encouraged from a young age to *not* react. Walk away. Don't fight back. Ignore them and they'll go away. Therefore, we often end up playing the whole thing out in our heads.

No one ever says, 'These people are slowing down your train of awesome, be sure to karate chop the crap out of them.'

Because – as we all know – no one actually speaks like that. . . . BUT sometimes your train doesn't feel so good and there's a few passengers on there that need dropping off.

You see, the truth is, growing up isn't always fun. It sounds sad but part of the teenage journey is realising a lot of your friends aren't really your friends. And of all the times I could've learned this, it had to be now. It hurt.

To be excluded is hard. Gradually becoming rejected by lifelong friends well and truly broke my heart.

It left me feeling out of place, uncomfortable in my own skin, and I couldn't seem to shift the sadness. The more I tried, the worse I felt. I stopped sleeping. Worry became a permanent feature.

'Friends come and go like waves of the ocean, but the true ones stick like an octopus on your face.'

—*Anon*

What made it all worse is that in fact I had no idea why this was happening. This was meant to be the best year yet. Why would someone do this to me?

But the beautiful thing is that bullies never win. It might feel like they do but in time it all comes back to haunt them. There's always a day of reckoning for them. Liars will always be found out. The truth will always win.

And it did, eventually.

But for months I was lost and I was lonely. I learned there is nothing worse than feeling left out. Because then 'they' come. The voices in my head. The self-doubt, the overthinking, the anxieties. For anyone out there reading this that knows what I'm talking about, you'll know it always hits harder at night. By 17, I'd been in school almost my entire life and no one had ever taught me how to deal with this.

Like most 17-year-olds, I bottled it all up and tried to 'fix' what was going on. My parents knew something was wrong. I had changed. I wasn't eating as much as normal, I was on edge and I was tired all the time.

Mum knew. Mums always know. And one day she sat me down and said, 'these are the people who think you're better than them, and they can't take it.'

And then it all came out. We spoke about it for hours. I cried a lot. Months of worry, hurt, fear, stress, sadness and confusion just poured out of me.

'You can't stop people from saying bad things about you. All you can do is make them liars.'

—Thomas Sowell

I think the thing I remember most from that conversation is that it's always useful to remember that not everyone is going to like or love you. Most people don't even like or love themselves. And why would you want everyone to like you when you don't even like everyone!

It has left me always double checking my own behaviour to make sure I never ever make someone feel the way I felt.

I remember wishing I had spoken to my parents sooner. Talking about exams was one thing but, as we all know, when it comes to talking about our feelings and our emotions, it's just so horrifically awkward.

I had felt like this before but not to this extent and not for this long. This was different, I couldn't shake it. My parents gave it a name: Anxiety.

Dear Parents,

"Because I said so" is not an acceptable answer to any question whatsoever.

Doesn't even make sense.

Kind regards,

Your Teenager

Confidently Lost

So many things are quick to be given a label nowadays, especially feelings and emotions we don't like. But we don't always get it right. Being heartbroken when someone splits up with you doesn't automatically mean you suffer from depression. You feeling alienated when someone tells you that your top is hideous doesn't mean you suffer from anxiety. The term 'mental health' is thrown about a lot, but there is a definite difference between being mentally ill and being mentally unhealthy.

The point I am making is that we are often quick to forget that negative and uncomfortable feelings are a hugely important part of life. Believe it or not, we need sadness. Without it, happiness would have no meaning. As weird as it may seem, sadness helps and guides us through so many emotional journeys in life. In fact, let's go further; sadness is vital to our mental health. Along with other things such as anger, research shows us that experiencing and accepting such emotions are key to our happiness.

I mentioned Disney movies earlier on. I'm sure you've seen *Inside Out*. If not, get it watched. It is the perfect reminder that Joy, Fear, Anger, Disgust and Sadness all live together within us, and it's all controlled by the 'you' in charge of your brain.

The world tells us from a young age that we should be happy. Could it be we've got it so wrong that by forcing a culture of happiness we breed unhappiness? Maybe we need to get better at being unhappy?

Being heartbroken sucks. Falling out with your best mate sucks. Being lonely sucks. Failing sucks. Being criticised sucks. Adolescence sucks.

But all the awful, negative feelings that we feel, all the crazy emotions that come to the surface make us better, stronger and yes, believe it or not, happier.

We all know it's hard to talk about feelings, especially in our teens. We'd much rather deal with these things on our own than with our parents. But remember, your parents have been there, they get it. No one is asking you to have a full on, in-depth conversation with them, but even a brief chat can make a huge difference.

Along with acceptance, sex, money, body image, embarrassment, stress, social media, failure, climate change and what the future holds, one of the biggest things teenagers worry about most is anxiety.

And it just so happens nowadays people *are* talking about it. A lot. Even at 17 I didn't truly understand what anxiety was. It was never spoken about. We certainly weren't taught about it in school. It was like Starbucks back  in those days. We'd heard that America had loads but not so much here. Before we knew it, every single city and town had a Starbucks and everyone wanted a piece of it.

OMG! I've just realised anxiety is the new Starbucks. It's the new rock 'n' roll, everyone's talking about it. We hear more about it than ever before and it would seem that everyone's joining in. It's in, it's fashionable, it's trendy and it's on every street corner!

To be clear, I'm not belittling anyone who says they have anxiety, I'm glad people are talking about it. I wish they were talking about it more when I was your age. But before we go any further, I should point out that being anxious and having an anxiety disorder are not the same thing.

'What screws us up most in life is the picture in our head of how it's supposed to be.'

—Anon

Anxiety is one of the biggest assholes you will ever meet, but knowing a little more about it might just help you to deal with it better or to understand what a friend is experiencing.

Here's my top 3 takeaways.

First things first, anxiety sucks. Literally, it sucks the life out of me. It's exhausting and can kick my ass at any time, taking me from zero to terrified in seconds. It can ruin a perfect day, I feel it throughout my entire body, other people rarely understand, then I spend the next few days thinking about it over and over again, lying in my bed wide awake all night, convincing myself everything in life is terrible.

This is anxiety at its worst.

Secondly, anxiety is not worry. All my life I have been called a worrier. But worrying about something and having anxiety are not the same thing. Worry tends to be more focussed on thoughts in our heads, while we feel anxiety throughout our entire body. Worry is more specific. We worry about getting to school on time, but we feel anxious about the day ahead, a vaguer, more general concern.

While being worried can cause mild emotional distress, anxiety is simply much more powerful and disruptive. Worry is caused by more realistic concerns than anxiety. If you're concerned about getting grounded because you flunked a school project, you're worried. If you're concerned about getting grounded because your parents didn't ask you if you enjoyed your packed lunch, you're anxious.

Worry is way more controllable and talking ourselves out of anxiety is much harder; it lingers, unlike worry.

Thirdly, anxiety is normal. Like, really normal. I always try to remind myself that in life we need anxiety. It's part of what makes us human, it's there for a reason, it keeps us alive. The reality is that most people only ever have it on a low level but some of us have it real bad. Most of the time I have a low level but fairly frequently it flares up. In 1996, at 17 years of age, it blew up.

'Don't let anyone steal ya joy! There's always someone miserable trying to bring you down . . . you just wish them well and proceed on enjoying your life.'

—Missy Elliot

I have been learning to live with anxiety from the age of 5. But it really kicked my ass at 17. There was a lot going on considering it was meant to be 'the best year of my life'.

In the end it led me to make some big decisions in life and ultimately it put me on the path I'm on now. I decided I wanted out of my hometown. My hometown is beautiful and there's a lot of good people, but I had outgrown it. I learned over time this is ok. It was time to go, be me and find my people. University seemed like the best option for this.

My plan was as follows . . .

1. Find a course that excites me.
2. Find a university far away.
3. Pass my exams.
4. Leave.

The pressure really was now on.

On paper, it was a simple plan. But it can be difficult with a cloud hanging over you.

I learned a valuable lesson in my last year of school. No matter how hard you work, no matter how kind you are, no matter how good your intentions are, sometimes, sometimes your face simply doesn't fit.

So, I learned to just go crack on and make it work with my own face. Just one thing though. I had to learn to make peace with my anxieties. I had to learn to manage it, to accept it, to live with it.

This was made harder by the constant stream of 'what if's'.

What if I fail again?

What if I don't get into uni?

What if I'm stuck here forever?

What if I don't get into comedy?

What if?

What if?

What if?

With anxiety, the danger that is feared isn't normally imminent – it may not even be known or realistic. Look at my questions above. Most of these are based on the unknown. I was freaking out about things that hadn't even happened.

But it's who I am. It's in me, it's what makes me, me!

FRODO: I can't do this, Sam.

SAM: I know. It's all wrong. By rights we shouldn't even be here. But we are. It's like in the great stories, Mr Frodo. The ones that really mattered. Full of darkness, and danger, they were. And sometimes you didn't want to know the end, because how could the end be happy? How could the world go back to the way it was when so much bad had happened? But in the end, it's only a passing thing, this shadow. Even darkness must pass. A new day will come. And when the sun shines, it'll shine out the clearer. Those were the stories that stayed with you. That meant something. Even if you were too small to understand why. But I think, Mr Frodo, I do understand. I know now. Folk in those stories had lots of chances of turning back only they didn't. They kept going. Because they were holding on to something.

FRODO: What are we holding on to, Sam?

SAM: That there's some good in this world, Mr Frodo . . . and it's worth fighting for.

'Your mind is like this water, my friend. When it is agitated, it becomes difficult to see. But if you allow it to settle, the answer becomes clear.'

—Grand Master Oogway

I decided to focus on my schoolwork and my writing. I decided that a Primary School Teaching degree was a good route to go. It was creative, varied, it would give me an audience every day and most importantly I would be able to help others and make a difference.

I was given permission to volunteer a couple of days a week in some local primary schools. I loved it and very quickly I had found my purpose. Many of my worries began to lift. Don't get me wrong, I was still stressed out of my box at times but there was now a renewed sense of focus. I hung out with different people, hung out more with my parents, wrote more comedy sketches and I worked harder on my schoolwork than I had ever worked before. It was my ticket out.

I even met a girl . . . now that really was a surprise!

Before I knew it, exams were passed (just), my bags were packed and I was in the car with Mum and Dad as we headed to the other end of the country where I was to spend 4 of the best years of my life, make the best friends I could imagine and 18 months later, meet my future wife.

It was also where my comedy career was to begin. Perhaps not the most obvious career choice for someone as anxious as me but on stage I am at my happiest, everything feels a little safer up there.

Anxiety followed me everywhere I went but having blown up in my last year at school, I was – in the most part – able to keep a lid on it throughout my 4 years at uni. In fact, for 20 years I managed it really rather effectively.

It has continued to play a big – still very much unwanted – role in my life. As recently as 2018, more than 20 years later, I had my biggest run-in with anxiety to date. I wasn't well for months.

We live in times where we can be encouraged to toughen up, get over it or man up. I kept telling myself, 'You've got kids now Gav, a successful career, you're the guy who stands on stages around the world making people laugh and feel great, you're not meant to feel like this anymore, you can't let people see this side of you.'

Still worried about what others might think, at 38 years of age, I made a mistake, a mistake I'd made before, I kept it to myself, pretended everything was ok, and my brain broke.

For any of you reading this who worry, who feel they are struggling with their mental health, who feel anxious or who have anxiety, here is a letter.

Dear fellow overthinkers,

I worry about things. I get embarrassed and I feel anxious about things. Sometimes it can get a bit much and I feel overwhelmed. Then I start to worry about the fact I'm worrying! I don't sleep much, I feel like I'm going to explode and occasionally I cry about it.

That's right, I'm 42, married, I have 2 kids, I run my own business, I write books, I've performed stand-up comedy all over the world and yet, I worry about things.

It's not just you. You are not alone, there are literally millions of us who feel the way you are feeling right now. As weird as it sounds, you are normal. These feelings will lift, and they will pass. They might return but you will get better at accepting and embracing your anxieties. You will learn new tricks and tips to deal with it.

I've been a worrier since I was about 2 years old. Here's some of the things I've worried about in my life.

Doing poos

Falling down the toilet

The dark

Being alone

Thunder

Being ill

The doctor

Hospitals

Flying

Plane crashes

Escalators

Lifts

School

My Gran' s beard

Reading out loud in class

Hospitals

Geese

Horses

Bullies

War

My body

The way I look

My friends

What people think of me

Exams

Failing

Girls

Boys

Getting old

Social media

Cancer

Dying

My Job

Paying bills

Succeeding

Going bald

You'll see there's some things on my list that are definitely not worth worrying about but through life it's hard to predict what kind of things will lead to worrying.

But I've learned that the best thing to do if you're worried about something or not feeling like yourself is talk to someone about it. I know everyone says that but it's true. Talk to your parents, grandparents, friends, teachers or even your pets!

Let your down days in, embrace them, show them around, but be sure to show them the door.

Remember, most things turn out ok in the end. Give yourself a break and don't be so hard on yourself.

You are amazing and we're gonna be ok.

Your fellow overthinker,

Gavin

'If we are not regularly deeply embarrassed by who we are, the journey to self-knowledge hasn't begun.'

—Alain de Botton

Let me share my top 5 tips for tackling anxiety.

Basically, this next section should really be called 'Stuff to do when you feel like your world is caving in, you can't stop worrying and you feel like you're about to explode.'

Catchy huh?

So, here goes. . . .

Stuff to do when you feel like your world is caving in, you can't stop worrying and you feel like you're about to explode.

1. Find Your Shove

Everyone says it, few do it. Every mental health charity, every mental health spokesperson and every single mental health campaign tells us the same thing, TALK TO SOMEONE. And yet it's just so hard. It feels so embarrassing. The last thing you want to be is that negative person who no one wants to be around. But this is different, this is your health and wellbeing. This is your happiness, you're not being negative, you're reaching out for help. You will be amazed just how willing others are to help you during tough times.

I'm lucky I have my wife Ali. She's amazing. She listens *and* kicks my ass all at the same time. But kicks my ass in the most positive, loving and 'exactly what Gavin needs' kind of way. She picks me up and gives me just the right amount of 'shove' in the right direction.

Talk to someone. Sit with someone. Hug someone. Find those that will listen, pick you up and dust you down. Talk to those that will allow you to express exactly how you are feeling. It's not always the most obvious people, welcome them in.

It might be your parents, grandparents, carers, teachers, friends, or the wee woman in the post office. Ok, that last one is a little bit random. . . .

Notice the people who make an effort to stay in your life.

Friends are great, but only a select few will sit with you when you need it most.

2. Write It Down!

Nowadays we live in a digital world of to-do list apps and Google Docs. The 6,000-year-old practise of putting pen to paper is sadly losing its appeal.

Writing stuff down just helps. In my teens I filled notebooks with comedy sketches, stories *and*, well, my emotions. Just getting it out, getting it down on paper brings a sense of relief. But there's proper science behind this stuff.

If you don't write things down, your mind spends more time 'paper shuffling' and it creates its own anxiety.

Just like having too many internet tabs open on your laptop at once, sometimes it feels like your brain has done the same thing. It's often the result of trying to mentally juggle too many thoughts or tasks at the same time.

Your brain is like a hard drive. A multi-layered, super-epic, crazily complex hard drive. And to make matters worse, it lies to us. I'm sure we'd love to know that our brain is our friend, but it's not. It's tricking us all the time. Even in important moments, our brains are not as good at creating accurate memories as we think they are. There will be memories from your childhood that simply aren't true, but you remember them clearly.

Your brain can help you to convince yourself you were awesome at something when in actual fact you were rubbish. Or quite the opposite, it can make you feel like a fraud when in actual fact you are fully deserving of all the recognition you are receiving.

And of course, it can make you scared of things that will never happen, or at the very least are incredibly unlikely to happen. I used to have a fear of flying. I've never been scared of heart disease and yet I'm from Scotland. My chances of dying from heart disease are far higher than being in a plane crash. But hey, for a time I wasn't concerned about my diet but was entirely convinced I shouldn't be getting on a plane.

The Zeigarnik effect says we tend to hang on to things in our minds, if we don't finish what we start. Writing down your ideas, thoughts and emotions gets them out your head, freeing up your mental space. It allows your brain to unload some baggage, preventing you from crashing your own precious mental browser.

It might even help you to relax.

There's no notifications popping up to distract you. A proper physical notebook or journal means no emails pinging in, no Instagram updates and no phone calls. Your thumbs can have a rest from the endless scrolling.

You'll remember more. In 2014, the Association of Psychological Science reported that students who physically took notes received a memory boost – particularly when compared to those who took notes via a laptop.

You can write anything down. Bright ideas that pop into your head. Goals that you want to achieve today or for the week ahead. One-liner reminders. To-Do list. To-Done list. Your little nuggets of wisdom and 'ah-ha's'. All the things buzzing around in your brain. Anything keeping you up at night. Your hopes, your dreams, your goals, and aspirations. Your fears, anxieties and concerns. You get the idea.

Writing things down is a powerful and useful habit. Even if you throw it away, you still get the benefits.

Writing Challenge

I dare you to buy yourself a lovely new notepad. A proper one. One that takes your breath away when you see it. (Tweet me a picture please to @gavinoattes)

Ok, so here's your challenge to get you started. All I want you to do for one week is write a 3-word happy story to describe your day.

That's it, just 3 words. Just before bed, create quite literally a 3-word happy story about your day.

If you feel the need to keep writing, then I dare you to keep going.

---

3. I'm Having the Thought That

This is one of the best techniques I've ever come across for reducing anxiety and/or removing upsetting thoughts. I learned this from Russ Harris's wonderful book *The Happiness Trap*.

The human mind is such a skilled storyteller. Not only is it skilled in creating the story but it has the unique ability to tell us those stories all the time, forever. It never stops.

The problem for many of us is that the story isn't always the happiest of stories. Some of the daily themes can be rather unpleasant.

Harris teaches us that most psychological approaches regard negative stories as a major problem and make a big fuss about trying to eliminate them. We're told to rewrite the story, think more positively, make yourself busy and you'll be distracted and on it goes. But the negative story never really goes away.

What we need to do is acknowledge the story but don't give it the time and energy we perhaps would normally unknowingly allocate.

At the height of my anxiety, lying in my bed, eyes wide awake, craving sleep and my chest ready to explode I simply take the negative thought I'm having, e.g. I'm never going to be able to sleep again, and focus on it for about 10 seconds. Next I take that thought and simply add to it 'I'm having the thought that . . . I'm never going to be able to sleep again. I then run it again and instantly I can feel a lifting. Then I do the same again but this time it's slightly longer: 'I notice I'm having the thought that I'm never going to sleep again.' Again, a further lifting. A distance is felt.

It really works for me, but it takes practice. Try it now. You'll find in time you are less likely to beat yourself up over negative thoughts and feelings. Remember, thoughts become things. This was a turning point for me. Practise practise practise.

'Anxiety is nothing but repeatedly reexperiencing failure in advance. What a waste.'

—Seth Godin

4. Goals Really Do Come True

Goal setting . . . I know, YAWNFEST! But trust me, I've got an immense technique for you that really works. In our teens we can get so wrapped up in the future, but this is all about the present and can help to reduce our worries. But before we get to it, let's talk about laughing at inappropriate times.

Have you ever laughed so hard it hurts? Isn't it just wonderful? Have you ever laughed so hysterically you can barely speak, there's tears, snot, you pee a little and you've forgotten how to breathe?

Again, wonderful. Well not the pee part, obvs.

But have you ever done it at a time you shouldn't? Isn't it just awful? You can't stop. You don't even know why you're laughing, and you're trying so hard not to, but it's happening anyway. It's even worse if your friend is in the room. You know not to look at them or it will get worse. But you can't help yourself, can you? You catch their eye and that's it, game over!

Your teacher is in mid flow, making the most serious of points and someone farts. You've heard a million farts but for some reason there's never been a funnier fart than this one. You say nothing, you stare right at the front of the classroom. Wasn't even that good a fart but for whatever reason, you just can't hold it back. No one else has even flinched. Did anyone else even hear it? You look to your left and catch your friend's eye. . . . Their face tells you they clearly heard it and that look is enough to tip you over the edge. You're gone.

Funerals are the worst. Funny stories are often shared but it's that weird uncomfortable feeling of 'am I meant to laugh at this?' that makes us laugh more than normal. It's a funeral, every bone in our body tells us we shouldn't be laughing. This is a sad, sombre occasion. But once you start, sometimes there's just no stopping.

I often think that this makes it harder sometimes to control our laughter. The tone of the event, or the environment we happen to be in can often dictate a seriousness in the room. We just know, don't we, that it's not a time for laughter. It's a time for manners, respect and sensibleness.

And this just makes it worse. . . .

A few years ago, I was at an awards night. A proper fancy type of affair with canapes, bubbly and bow ties. I don't own a bow tie, I had to opt for the second-class regular tie. In the room were some of the most successful people in the world. A who's who of the business community. It felt very professional, very serious and grown up.

I felt very nervous and very out of place and, to add to this, I was up for an award. This was a big deal to me and there were huge cash prizes up for grabs for those with the best business ideas.

Like all award nights, there was a special guest, and this particular guest had been the successful recipient of the top prize from the previous year. His business was awarded a six-figure sum that had transformed his business and rightly so he was there to share his incredible journey of how the prize money was used to develop a brand new and extraordinary piece of technology that will revolutionise the world of engineering.

I'm not going to lie, I barely understood a word he said. A cracking guy with a cracking business but it was all flying *way* over the top of my head. Hundreds of people around the room appeared to be hanging onto every word he said. I'm sure it was all hugely impressive but it's not my thing and the words he was saying were all blurring into one great big technology themed, intellectually-too-much-for-me presentation that left me feeling entirely out my depth. My imposter syndrome was in full flow!

And then something happened.

He said the words, 'reverse pumping'.

Well . . .

Everything went into slow motion.

I didn't know where to look so I looked down at my feet.

Then he said it again, 'reverse pumping'.

And again.

I don't care how childish this sounds. I understand he had a context. But in this moment, this was the funniest thing that I had ever heard.

He kept saying it, 'reverse pumping'.

All I could think was 'stop saying it, please stop saying it'.

In huge, big colourful letters it appeared on the screen. Each letter about a metre tall, REVERSE PUMPING.

My entire body was going into some kind of pre-laughter spasm. I was visibly shaking; I could barely breathe.

All I heard next was 'Teaching others to reverse pump'. Again, I was aware of other words being said but it was like my brain was deliberately shutting them out, once again ignoring the context.

'The benefits of reverse pumping' came next, and it was here I made a schoolboy error.

I turned and I looked at my business partner and yes, eye contact was made.

I was gone.

Have you ever tried to laugh uncontrollably in silence? Of course you can't, it's uncontrollable. I nearly slipped a disc.

This is the very type of laughter that earns you looks of absolute disgust, the type of laughter that ensures you're never invited back again. People were pointing. I had to leave and go for some fresh air.

Looking back on it, it's still funny but it's not *that* funny. It was just one of those moments that catches you out unexpectedly and it snowballs beyond belief. I actually met the guy later that evening and congratulated him on his success. He was genuinely fascinating and taught me that sometimes by reversing things, we gain a different perspective and therefore we find solutions and achieve results we might never have experienced had we followed traditional methods.

And believe it or not, I had a bit of a moment and his words have stuck with me. Not the pumping part, the reverse part, and this leads me to my next point, and just a heads-up, it's another biggie. . . .

Goal setting. *Reverse* goal setting to be exact. Not nearly as funny as reverse pumping but this will change your life.

You Don't Have to Wait for Anything

'There is no elevator to success, you have to take the stairs.'

—*Anon*

We've already covered my support for being a dreamer. But dreams don't come true without getting off your backside and making them happen.

You could say dreams are the easy part. And they're free too! But remember, they're imaginary, so we need the goals to make the wonderful visions in your head become real. It's the goals that get us results.

Dreams are mega important, they inspire us, but it's the goals that bring the focus to change our lives.

Goal setting is massive. It's an industry in itself. Google alone lists over 20 million results for 'goal setting'. There are books dedicated to this stuff. Planners, worksheets, coaches, articles and residential experiences aimed at perfecting our techniques. In turn there are millions upon millions of us trying to achieve them.

One of the biggest problems with goal setting is that most people fail. They have a cost: time, money, effort, sweat, tears and sometimes your friends. If we were successful, we'd all be healthy, wealthy, happy, fulfilled and there would be way less mental health problems. Our yachts would line the streets because our waterways would be full of our other yachts.

We are forever asked questions such as: Where do you see yourself in 5 years? What do you want to have achieved in life by the time you retire? It's all very future focussed and, at times, mega stressful!

The challenge with the 5 years/10 years type of questioning is that 'you' 5 to 10 years from now will be a very different 'you' to right now.

But there's hundreds of versions of this! 1 year from now, 5 years, 10 years, 20 years, on and on it goes. We just keep moving the goalposts, climbing more ladders, striving, aiming, looking ahead, working for the future. Pressure, pressure and more pressure.

Don't worry about the future, it's got you covered. It's got its eye on you. Think about right now. It's hard to guess what will make us happy in 10 years. I'm willing to bet, though, that you know what would make you happy right now.

At 13 years of age we're asked to think about our career choices and choose school subjects that will put us on the right path. I can recall being asked in high school, 'Where do you see yourself in 20 years?' Really? I'm 13 mate, I'm just worried about how to get rid of my moobs and talk to girls right now.

Traditional goal setting is all about the future. Set a huge goal and break it down into manageable chunks. Start at the beginning and then lay it all out step by step, blah blah blah.

Sometimes it works.

Sometimes it works but each and every time a goal is achieved it's usually followed by '*whats next?*' It hasn't been 5 minutes and already we're moving on to the next goal. Goal setting can be extremely beneficial, but it can suck the joy out of the journey to the thing that's meant to make us happy and fulfilled.

The best example of this for me is my time doing comedy. Rather than enjoying the present I was becoming too wrapped up in what's next. Making it. What's bigger? What's better?

Would I rather be on that stage, giving it my all, completely and utterly in the moment, feeling great and not get a 5-star review . . . OR . . . be so laser-focused on getting a 5-star review that I lose sight of everything else, stressing myself in the process and not enjoy the performance at all?

Now when I'm on stage, my goal is simple; give it my best on that day and come off stage feeling good enough to want to do it all again tomorrow.

Too many of us spend our days feeling discouraged, tired or unmotivated from chasing an endless stream of goals that seem a long way away, so maybe it's time to re-examine the order of things. Or more so, our timescales.

So, what is reverse goal setting, why is it great and, more importantly, how do we do it?

This is about gaining a different perspective. Flipping the traditional on its head and seeing things through a slightly different lens. Inspired by my Reverse Pumping friend (still funny) and all sorts of experts like Benjamin Harvey, we spot different opportunities, find new solutions to problems and all sorts of goals will jump out along the way. Reverse goal setting is less about 'making it' in the old school sense and more about working out a path for yourself that is actually fulfilling, right now.

And best of all, it's really simple.

Ask yourself 3 questions.

1. What do I want to feel right now?
2. What activity can I do right now to give me that feeling?
3. If I do this activity regularly, what results would it create?

That's it! It's that simple and once you gain momentum with this you'll be amazed at just what you achieve.

Let me give you an example. You might say right now, '*I want to feel healthier*'. Ok, what activity allows you to do that? A 30-minute walk outdoors always leaves us feeling better both mentally and physically. So, today you will want to have a 30-minute walk round the block. If you did this every day for 6 weeks, what sort of result would that create?

It would create a healthier, happier you right from the off! So, if you want to be a healthier, happier you then commit to do something that builds momentum. Before you know it, a 30-minute walk might turn into a 60-minute walk. It might even turn into a run . . . and you might even end up running a marathon 2 years later, but from day 1 you felt better.

You might say, 'Right now, I would like to feel relaxed.' Magic! Today, what activity makes you relaxed? You might say, '15 minutes of mindfulness makes me feel relaxed, every time I do it, it chills me out a little.' Awesome. So, if you do 15 minutes of mindfulness every day for the rest of your life, what sort of results would that create? There's going to be a far less stressed you walking about and, who knows, you might just become a mindfulness master in the process! Imagine how many goals you'll achieve being more relaxed!

Why wait 10, 20, 30, 40, 50 years to truly start living? There's no point. You don't have to wait for anything. You can feel the way you want to feel today. You don't have to postpone you. You don't have to put you off.

No more constant chasing, wishing and hoping for stuff that feels like a lifetime away. Right now, choose the feelings you want to feel, find the activities that give you these feelings and do them.

That's it – 3 simple steps. Boom.

5. Breathe (Possibly the Most Important One)

Seriously, remember to breathe. Not breathing is the number one cause of death. Be sure to keep it going. A good deep breath can fix many a broken thought.

CHAPTER

Once Upon a Time, the End

> *'Some of us aren't meant to belong. Some of us have to turn the world upside down and shake the hell out of it until we make our own place in it.'*
>
> —*Elizabeth Lowell*

You'll notice the next page is blank. Grab yourself a pen or a pencil. Don't worry, I'm not about to ask you to do loads of writing!

All I need you to do is write down the 5 things you value most in life. I don't want to give you examples as this needs to come from you. But it can literally be anything.

Take a few minutes, scribble your thoughts down and we'll come back to this shortly.

Is It a Bird? Is It a Plane? No, It's You, You Legend!

They say all good things must come to an end. You, me, this book, everyone and everything. Except LEGO, obviously. It's made of plastic and will literally be here forever.

I actually love LEGO. It's remarkable the hours that can go into it. I must have clocked up months of playing with the stuff. It a huge investment. Yes, financially but more so time, energy and effort. It's very similar to life.

Think about it. For all the joy and fun LEGO can bring us, it can bring pain and anguish too. In fact, there's only one thing more painful than stepping on LEGO and that's *kneeling* on LEGO! Fact! But it's true, life can be painful too.

'LEGO', in Danish, actually means 'play well' and, as we all know, life is best lived when it's played well. LEGO sometimes comes in a massive box of random bits. You tip them out onto the carpet and start creating something amazing. LIFE's also like that, you have to piece the bits together to create something amazing, weird or random. LEGO is about building. LIFE is about building (friendships, knowledge, skills, interests, abilities, experience . . . *ourselves*).

But sometimes LEGO isn't random. It comes in a kit. You open it up and the bits are grouped in little bags with numbers on them. There's a picture and a plan. It's quite complicated, it takes a while and you might need someone to help, but if you stick with it, you will end up with something that looks a bit like the picture on the box. For some people, life can be like that. They have an idea in their mind about what they want to achieve – a goal, a dream, an ambition – and if they stick at it and follow the instructions, they'll achieve it in the end. Or something that looks a bit like it. Plus, life is always easier when others help out with the tricky bits.

Life is a gift. It was given to you by your parents. If you haven't thanked them for it, please do. Quite often, LEGO is also a gift. More likely a birthday prezzie from your Aunty Susan. She needs thanking too.

You think LEGO has some random characters? It's got nothing on life!

It's okay to start over. Sometimes, you get it right; sometimes you don't. With LEGO and life, the aim is to learn from your attempts, mistakes and failures, and *keep on building*.

LEGO can be messy. As can life. Sometimes it's all about the tidy up. A clear out. Repackaging can be healthy. And then passing it on to someone else feels great.

The truth is, we're all just kind of making it up. It's a huge secret that most people don't tell you. No one really 100% knows what they're doing 100% of the time.

'Sometimes you make the story up as you go along and have no idea how it will come out.'

—*Ernest Hemingway*

I'm old enough to remember the days when LEGO used to claim that a free dinosaur came with every pack, sometimes a free airplane. Very clever marketing when you think about it!

Life is an enormous box of LEGO. But with it comes a free YOU. Better than any dinosaur or airplane. And you can build your free YOU any way, shape or size you want. You can add pieces, change parts, start over and learn a million lessons along the way.

But remember, there are billions of pieces. Life is often complicated, as hard as we try to manage all the pieces, life – or LEGO for that matter – is rarely simple. But when we stick at it, try new things, have the courage to fail and start again, when it works it's a magical thing.

And just like in life, there's always easier routes and safer options. There's always DUPLO. It's not nearly as exciting and you definitely won't get it stuck up your nose!

Very few of us have a full LEGO set still fully built and in one piece. Like life, a piece will fall out from time to time, or we lose a key piece that holds everything (or everyone) together.

Everything Comes and Goes

Let's talk about endings. We experience what Frank Ostaseski calls 'little deaths' almost daily. We might lose a piece of jewellery, a key, money, a shoe, anything really.

But you know and I know, it's not just 'little deaths', unfortunately loss comes in all shapes and sizes.

It can be job shaped, relationship shaped, confidence shaped, freedom shaped, dream shaped, pet shaped, everything shaped.

Even phone shaped.

Phone shaped?

Yeah.

Imagine the scenario. . . .

It's a Friday evening. You're thinking about heading out to meet some friends but you're running a little late. You know there's a party happening, you're just about to find out where and boom. . . .

Your phone freezes . . . and then it switches off. It won't come back on. It flickers . . . and dies.

Your phone is dead.

Many of us know how this feels, it's not just a spanner in the works, this is an entire bag of spanners in life. It sucks and it's often followed by the 5 stages of phone grief:

1. **WTAF?** – Your first reaction is of horror and disbe-
   lief. You cannot believe this is happening to you
   when you are already running late. You try to
   start the phone again and again and again.
   Charger is in, you're holding down buttons for
   15 seconds. You know the drill. Aaargh!

2. *Raging* – Now that you realise the phone cannot be switched on, you can feel your blood boiling. *All* the swear words fly through your head. It's clearly your parents' fault as they bought you

the phone in the first place. Your friends are probably trying to call you. You're going to miss the party. . . . FOMO is kicking off, right?

3. **Hostage Situation** – Even though you know it won't help, and it's a little weird, you start talking to your phone like it's a hostage situation! It's negotiation time. You're asking it nicely to start, just once. You tell it you'll keep it maintained, get the battery charged as soon as possible and love it forever. You're making promises that you know you can't keep as you pat it gently.

4. **Totes Pressed** – You basically turn into Eeyore. All the negative thoughts start rushing to your mind. You begin to feel depressed, sad and hopeless. You see no way out of the situation. Your life is ruined. It's over. Just what will people say? You could cry. It's the end of the world.

5. **Frustreptance** – Levels of frustration are high but you're beginning to accept the situation. After a firm talking to from your own self, you figure out what you should do next. Your mum has your mate's mum's number. Easy, you just call her, explain what's happened, she gives you the details and texts your mate to let them know you're going to be late. Sorted.

Or, worse case, you can't get your phone working, your mum doesn't have your mate's mum's number, you have no other way of communicating so you can't go to the party. Tough! You take it on the chin, and you get over it. You'll live. Life goes on.

Unfortunately, there's not just 'little deaths'. There's also 'XL deaths'. These too come in all shapes and sizes.

And every now and then, they're human shaped.

'Death is a challenge. It tells us not to waste time.'

—*Leo Buscaglia*

Factor 50

There was some amazing music around when I was your age. So many new bands and so many great tunes that caught the mood of our teenage years.

It's now over 20 years since Baz Luhrmann gave the world the hugely inspirational 'Everybody's Free'. You may know it better as the 'Wear Sunscreen' song.

Released in 1999, the song – originally an essay by Mary Schmich – gave us various bits of advice on how to live our best life and avoid all the nonsense that gets in the way of experiencing happiness.

With lyrics inspiring us to enjoy our youth, to imagine, to worry less, to remember compliments and forget insults, 'Everybody's Free' moved a generation to dance, to NOT read beauty magazines and to do something each day that scares us. It encouraged us to travel, to be patient and to remember that while friends will come and go, we need to hold on to the precious few.

I wonder if we were to rewrite this song for today how different it would be. If there was ever a time we needed this type of anthem to energise our world, it's now.

There are many lines in this song I'd keep the same and probably a few I'd like to add for modern times. Perhaps right at the start we could add 'Put your phone down.'

But 20 years since its release I can absolutely say with confidence that we *are* reading far too many beauty magazines, we are absolutely *not* dancing enough and we are certainly not patient enough.

There's more worry in the world than ever and everyone is **not** free; free to love who they want, travel where they want, look how they want, be who they want to be.

But the one line I always remember most and yet never fully appreciated until much later was **'Get to know your parents, you never know when they'll be gone for good.'**

I still remember the day like it was yesterday – 20th March 2012, recognised globally as International Day of Happiness. A day that was chosen to represent all that is good in the world, designed by governments around the world to *'dedicate our efforts to filling our world with happiness'*.

It's also the day my dad died.

Of all the days to die, he only went and died on the happiest day of the year. Whilst definitely ironic, there's also something very cool about this. Happiness and loss don't normally go together.

My dad was magic, the funniest human you could ever meet and we were really close. But he died too young and I wasn't prepared for what came next. Losing a phone feels like a kick in the teeth, it's a 'little death', but this, this was a sucker punch, it was 'extra large'. And even years later, it hurts every single day.

It's called grief.

Nothing. Stays. The. Same

I have spoken and written about losing my dad a lot. I'm beginning to learn that it's been my way of dealing with it and my way of keeping my dad alive.

I've had many conversations with many teenagers about loss. I've shared my experience of grief with thousands of people all over the world, but never have I been able to sum it up so succinctly as G. Snow did on Reddit a few years back.

So, for those of you who have experienced loss, those that are grieving, those that know it's coming or those worried about losing someone close to you. Read this. Read it twice if you must. It's perfect.

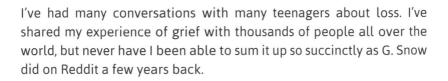

'Alright, here goes. I'm old. What that means is that I've survived (so far) and a lot of people I've known and loved did not. I've lost friends, best friends, acquaintances, co-workers, grandparents, mom, relatives, teachers, mentors, students, neighbours, and a host of other folks. I have no children, and I can't imagine the pain it must be to lose a child. But here's my two cents.

I wish I could say you get used to people dying. I never did. I don't want to. It tears a hole through me whenever somebody I love dies, no matter the circumstances. But I don't want it to 'not matter'. I don't want it to be something that just passes. My scars are a testament to the love and the relationship that I had for and with that person. And if the scar is deep, so was the love. So be it.

Scars are a testament to life. Scars are a testament that I can love deeply and live deeply and be cut, or even gouged, and that I can heal and continue to live and continue to love. And the scar tissue is stronger than the original flesh ever was. Scars are a testament to life. Scars are only ugly to people who can't see.

As for grief, you'll find it comes in waves. When the ship is first wrecked, you're drowning, with wreckage all around you. Everything floating around you reminds you of the beauty and the magnificence of the ship that was, and is no more. And all you can do is float. You find some piece of the wreckage and you hang on for a while. Maybe it's some physical thing. Maybe it's a happy memory or a photograph. Maybe it's a person who is also floating. For a while, all you can do is float. Stay alive.

In the beginning, the waves are 100 feet tall and crash over you without mercy. They come 10 seconds apart and don't even give you time to catch your breath. All you can do is hang on and float. After a while, maybe weeks, maybe months, you'll find the waves are still 100 feet tall, but they come further apart. When they come, they still crash all over you and wipe you out. But in between, you can breathe, you can function. You never know what's going to trigger the grief. It might be a song, a picture, a street intersection, the smell of a cup of coffee. It can be just about anything . . . and the wave comes crashing. But in between waves, there is life.

Somewhere down the line, and it's different for everybody, you find that the waves are only 80 feet tall. Or 50 feet tall. And while they still come, they come further apart. You can see them coming. An anniversary, a birthday, or Christmas, or landing at O'Hare. You can see it coming, for the most part, and prepare yourself. And when it washes over you, you know that somehow you will, again, come out the other side. Soaking wet, sputtering, still hanging on to some tiny piece of the wreckage, but you'll come out.

Take it from an old guy. The waves never stop coming, and somehow you don't really want them to. But you learn that you'll survive them. And other waves will come. And you'll survive them too. If you're lucky, you'll have lots of scars from lots of loves. And lots of shipwrecks.'

The professionals will sum this up as the '5 stages of grief'. Shock and Denial – Anger – Bargaining – Depression – Acceptance.

Looks a little similar to the 5 stages of phone grief, right? Losing a phone is awful. We've all been there. But when we lose a loved one, the pain we experience can feel unbearable. Understandably, grief is complicated, and we sometimes wonder if the pain will ever end.

It's important to note that the 5 stages of grief are not always experienced in the same order. Some fly through them, others bounce around between them for some time. I went through them all. Add to this shock, loneliness, sadness, guilt and anxiety. It's hugely overwhelming and confusing at the time. It doesn't feel normal, but it is.

Losing a human sucks. But I'm reminded of a quote from 'Tuesdays with Morrie' that reads 'Death ends a life but it doesn't end a relationship'. I lost my dad a good few years ago now. Do I still think about him? Every day. Does it still hurt? Most days. Do I still talk to him? All the time. Do I still get upset? Yeah. Is that normal? Of course it is.

Good Grief

But I also experienced the upward turn. This is an important moment when living with grief. Things feel a little lighter, easier almost.

Through my own experiences and through all my conversations with others, one of the biggest lessons I have learned about grief is that it can be good for us.

Loss is difficult to deal with but sometimes it can give new energy to life and bring awareness we have been needing to make some changes. It can spark new beginnings.

I know it's a cliché but I almost immediately thought about how short and precious life is. So many things that used to irritate and stress me out just vanished, I felt a sense of relief, freer almost. Losing my dad inspired me to re-evaluate what's important to me. I took up running, I ate healthier, and I spent more time with my family. Funnily enough, the time I lost my phone felt similar. I felt freer and spent more time with my family.

Weirdly, it's a bit like so many people's COVID experiences. Millions of us sitting about the house grieving for our past lives, our freedoms that we were so used to. COVID forced us all to re-evaluate, re-think and re-imagine life.

People reconnected through Zoom with others they hadn't seen for years, they got fit, they got healthy, they learned new skills, they fell back in love with the outdoors, they remembered who they were and what mattered.

Of course, this wasn't the same for everyone, some experienced nothing but loneliness, stress and anxiety. I get that but I'm keen to highlight that even loss and grief can cause a positive ripple in our lives. It can be hard to see but it's there and it's worth looking for.

Through grief we learn so much about love, care and support. We can find new energy and a determination to help others in a similar situation. It can shape us, bring us focus and a new sense of gratitude. It can even set you on a new career path!

Yes, it might just consume your entire being for a while, but it will remind you to live your life and surround yourself with the best humans. It *will* make you stronger, more resilient and you'll probably end up a better person!

Famous Last Words

I got the phone call at 6 am. It was my mum and it was grave. 'You need to come now.' I had known for some time this call was coming and yet I still wasn't prepared. Are we ever really prepared for that call?

The doctor wasn't expecting my dad to last much longer, so I needed to get to the hospital. And fast. I was due to be giving a speech that morning at a school in the Scottish Borders. I had to phone a colleague and tell him what was happening, he told me to get off the phone and go, he'd take care of things at work. I hung up the phone and as I turned around my wife Ali handed me a bag with a few items of clothing and some toiletries. 'Just go.' I hugged her and ran out the door.

My dad had been rushed to a hospital two hours from where I live. My biggest fear was that I wouldn't make it in time to say goodbye. A few speed limits broken, I made it to the hospital, parked up and ran past the phalanx of pyjama-clad smokers, some with drips attached to their arms. I continued to sprint along hospital corridors, following the blue line, up three flights of stairs towards Ward 8. Double doors ahead, I stopped and sucked in a few lungfuls of air. I knew that on the other side of those doors was my absolute hero, my best friend, my dad. And I was about to see him for the last time.

My brother had got there before me. He and my mum sat in silence. They left the room and gave me time to sit and speak with Dad. Pumped full of morphine and with very shallow breathing, he was completely unresponsive. I didn't care. I said all the things I wanted to say and kissed him on the forehead.

Hours passed. Dad remained unconscious.

Several hours later, having been sat around him sharing memories and telling stories from years gone past, my dad's eyes shot open. He lifted his head off the pillow, looked at mum, looked at my brother, turned to me and said . . .

'What the f**k's going on?'

He closed his eyes and slipped away.

Those were his very last words, and I reckon they're perfect. I shared that story at his funeral, except I didn't bleep the f-word. Even the minister laughed. I can hear dad saying it now as I type this.

He's the coolest dad in the world, right to the very end. I don't want to overanalyse his immortal last sentence, but could it be that my old man, who I assumed knew everything about everything, knew nothing about anything?

It's generally accepted that life is not a rehearsal. This may explain why a lot of people seem to be making a total hash of it. They're just making it up as they go along. What if we're all just bumbling along in the dark?

Look around, the world is bonkers. Nothing but uncertainty!

So just what is going on? I think the short answer to that is nobody actually knows.

But, one thing is definitely certain. You are alive. And as we established right at the start, lucky to be so. Well then, for as long as you get to stay alive, you might as well gie it laldy.

GIE IT LALDY

Verb

1. **To give one's all, to be very vigorous or energetic**
2. **To sing or do proudly, with great gusto**

To give something laldy is the daily life equivalent of 'dance like no one is watching'. To be in the moment, carefree and generally just giving it all you've got. But with a smile on your face and not a care for what others think! Although, to be fair, they're probably not watching, they'll be too busy scrolling. . . .

'Give the world the best you have and you'll get kicked in the teeth. Give the world the best you have anyway.'

—Kent M. Keith

Far too many of us are spending our time agonising over all the stuff that doesn't matter and worrying about fitting in. Fit out for a change. It's not about how busy we can be, what you look like or who makes the most money. It's not about the size of your house or who drives the fanciest car. Guess what? No one cares! Literally, at the end of the day, no one gives a 'flying monkey's'.

To Not Give a Monkey's

Verb

1. **To be disinterested or indifferent**
2. **To not care**

 When you die none of this will be discussed at your funeral. People will be too busy discussing what kind of human you were. And I can tell you right now, you'll either be remembered as one of the good guys or an asshole.

'I realised that I don't have to be perfect. All I have to do is show up and enjoy the messy, imperfect, and beautiful journey of my life.'

—*Kerry Washington*

Life? Completed It Mate!

Need, Need, Need, Need, Need . . .

I remember as a young kid being obsessed with sticker albums. It was so exciting when my dad brought home the latest one, the buzz of going to the wee shop to get packets of stickers, only to tear them open was just pure magic. The goal was always to fill the album as quickly as possible, so I was first to be able to say 'completed it!' The race was always on.

We would spend every ounce of our pocket money, no matter how little we had, on those stickers. It's an expensive business! More often than not, it was football stickers. I don't even like football. But like millions of other wee kids, I was obsessed with collecting these sticky treasures. From the highs of finding a 'shiny' to the crushing lows of discovering your pal had a 'double' of the sticker you needed most, but wouldn't do 'swapsies' with you. It had it all.

Every day at school and every day straight after school; need, need, need, need, need, need, need, need, need, need, need, need, need, need, need, need, need, need, need, got, need, need, need, need, need, need. . . .

I never completed one. Ever. Very few people do. Like many things growing up, it's usually a short-lived fad. Or we keep getting the same stickers, the 'swap' pile grows exponentially, and we lack the highly sought-after glittery ones. It can get repetitive, frustrating, boring even, we get distracted, jealousy creeps in, others get there first, they're collection is bigger, better and their parents buy them more, so we move on to something else.

There were always rumours that someone had completed it. Never saw any proof so in my head it didn't happen. I reckon no one ever truly completes a sticker album. I really wanted to though, more than anything, was that too much to ask?

So often I wished I'd never started!

The attic in my mum's house most likely has a box of nearly completed sticker albums. Everything from World Cups to Transformers to the Olympics. None of them full.

Sounds a bit like life, no one ever completes it. It's like the internet, you can't finish it, there's simply too much to do, too much to see. Yes, life is full of glittery prizes but there's just too many 'shiny's' to collect. And it always feels like there's someone who has nailed it and has it all. They've 'completed it!'

But that's part of the problem for so many. It's always been the problem. The race is on, a constant search for the big prize of being first, constantly seeking the glittery moments, craving what others have, the dream car, the promotion, the mansion, prepared to swap it all just to be the first to say 'completed it'. . . and then probably post it on Instagram.

Need, need, need, need, need, need, need, need, need, need, need, need, need, need, need, need, need, need, need, got, need, need, need, need, need, need . . .

In life, the things we think we need are usually things we want. We really don't need very much.

The only finish line in life is death and I'm not sure about you but I'm definitely not keen on finishing. There's so much to learn and so much to do, you can't possibly do it all. By all means ram your life full and live life to the max but one of the biggest lessons we can learn is to be grateful for what/who we *do* have rather than spend all our time thinking about what we *don't* have.

I'm just like you are. I enjoy collecting experiences, new memories and making new friends.

And if you're one of *those* types, always chasing the next big shiny prize then there's no shinier prize than your happiness. And we all know the things that make us happy aren't things.

 Life isn't for completing. It's for living.

Here's to being happily unfinished.

Dear Parents,

When was the last time you caught your kids doing something AMAZING... and then told them about it?

Kind regards,

Teenagers

x

What's the Story?

'The one who follows the crowd will usually go no further than the crowd. Those who walk alone are likely to find themselves in places no one has ever been before.'

—*Albert Einstein*

I called it at the start of this book. Born, live, die. Only two out of three guaranteed. A life and death sandwich. But what kind of sandwich are you building for yourself? What's in the middle? Is your filling of choice all you had hoped?

You see, the middle is the bit that's up for grabs. The filling is life itself. And truly living life to the full is not always guaranteed or definite. We all like different fillings but the most exciting part is you get to choose your own. Over time you begin to understand what you like, what works for you, what you want more of and what makes you want to puke. You get a little more daring and adventurous with your filling and sometimes all we want is 'just ham' or 'just cheese', which is fine if you want a dull sandwich. But if life's a sandwich – and you're the sandwich maker – why not fill it with epic ingredients?

If your sandwich is rubbish, or not exciting enough, or full of cucumber, why not start experimenting? Adjust the filling, try something new, discover new flavours, drop the bland, upgrade the ingredients.

From a young age we are taught that every great story has a beginning, a middle and an end. We always remember the ending. But just like a great sandwich, we need middles.

It's where the bulk of the story rests. It holds the reader's attention, but most importantly it is where we reach the climax or turning point of the story. The middle is just as important as the beginning and the end. If the middle is delicious, the reader will remain invested.

My friend is a novelist and she told me all about the 'sagging middle', an issue that novelists work hard to avoid as they construct their story. Sounds like something I face when I don't exercise enough!

Remember, though, the middle is the hard part. It's the bit where you need to actually live. To combat a 'sagging middle' requires more energy than normal but it's entirely worth the effort. And then when we get to the end of our story, there's no looking back with regret.

I remember conversations with my dad about all the things he was planning to do with his life. But cancer was to deny him of these. There's a tonne of books out there highlighting the regrets that adults have towards the end of their life. I wonder if you can guess what people's biggest ones are?

In a nutshell – based on years of brilliant research by Bronnie Ware – the top 5 regrets of the dying are:

1. **Not being true to self**
2. **Working too hard**
3. **Not having the courage to express feelings**
4. **Losing touch with great friends**
5. **Not letting happiness in more often**

Not being true to yourself is literally the number one regret of the dying. In other words, living a life of fitting in, conforming, being society and doing what is expected by others. But this is not just something people feel at the end of their lives. Some of us feel it throughout. Many of us feel it in our teens. We feel it in our bones, eating away at us as our dreams and ambitions are slowly replaced by what is considered normal. It's easier this way, less risk of ridicule, less risk of alienation, less risk of failure. And a lot less fun.

Number 5 is surprisingly common. So many of us don't realise until the end that happiness is a choice. Ware discovered through her research that the fear of change had many pretending to others and to themselves that they were content but the truth is *'many longed to laugh properly and have silliness in their life again'*.

Let's compare this to the findings of Dr Alastair McAlpine who spends every day caring for children with life-threatening and life-limiting illnesses. He asked his young terminally ill patients what they enjoyed most in life and what was most important to them.

Their list looked somewhat like this . . .

1. **Parents**
2. **Pets**
3. **Kindness**
4. **Laughing**
5. **Fun (toys, swimming and stories all regularly mentioned)**

But there was more.

Firstly, let's note that **NONE** of the adults *or* children said they wished they'd watched more TV and **NONE** said they should've spent more time on Facebook.

NONE regretted spending too little time online, **NONE** wished they'd had more Wi-Fi.

EVERYONE wished they'd worried less, and **ALL** spoke highly of music and ice-cream.

Lastly, perhaps most importantly, for both the adults *and* the children, **NOTHING** was more important than family. **NOTHING**.

Live Deliberately

Look back at your list from earlier, the one with the 5 things you value most in life. I have no idea what's on there and whilst it would be tough to guess your list word for word, I'm going to assume that 'my phone' isn't on your list. I'm going to assume 'trying to fit in' isn't on your list. I'm going to assume 'worrying about other people's opinions' isn't on your list and I'm going to assume that 'the way I look' isn't on your list. You get my point.

Therefore, I'm going to assume it includes things related to health, family, friends, time and fun. And yet so many of us give so much time and energy to the stuff that doesn't make us happy.

If health is at the top of your list, then how much time are you giving to it versus time spent scrolling?

If family is on your list, then how much time are you spending in your room, alone with your phone, versus chatting and laughing with your family?

Again, you get my point.

You live for about 28,000 days. You have literally tens of thousands of days, each one full of opportunities to go outside, take a deep breath and remember who you are. This is about having the courage to stand out. To be real. To build the best life sandwich you possibly can, making it as delicious as possible.

This is about choosing happiness. Deliberately.

Life stops for no one and, before you know it, you'll be looking back wondering just where the time went.

Speaking of time, I've probably taken up way too much of yours already. So, if you'd be so kind to let me summarise and I'll be on my way.

I thought about summing my book up like this. . . .

Stop Hitting Snooze. 7 years of brilliant and shite. Stop pretending to be normal. Laugh. Act your age, literally. Stay excited. Stay young. Be weird. Be brave. Be curious. Be courageous. Be flawed. Be scared. Believe. Ask questions. Ask for help. Say no. Dream. Burst with magic. Build dens. Jump in puddles. Positive vibes only. Play. Play with your food. Grow. Wonder. Wander. Imagine. Never fight a lion. Fail gloriously. Avoid the Kardashians (ok, this wasn't in the book). Don't be a dick. No wrong path. Turn up. Take part. Give a shit. Be kind. Phone down. Look up. Laugh. Keep swimming. Put the trolley away. Write. Move. Think about thinking. Different is cool. Share. Talk. Listen. Worry less. Look after your mental health. Family first. Good friends only. Be connected. Be silly. Talk. Offline. Turn the music up. Sing. Dance. You are not Beyoncé. Choose happiness. Ice cream helps. Eat your greens. Get a dog. Or a cat. Everything ends. No compare. Start over. Laugh. Fart. Hang out with your grandparents. Be real. Be you.

But . . . I feel like this would be the easy option. It's another list. Instead, however, I want to channel some inspiration from something that played a huge role in my teenage years.

We started with crisps in Chapter 1. I challenged you to treat this book as your metaphorical bag of crisps. To reach in and pull from it something the size of your face, that lifts you so much you need to go share it. We progressed to building the greatest sandwich you possibly could. Building a life for yourself that's as delicious as you can possibly make it.

I love sandwiches and crisps. And sandwiches with crisps. And crisp sandwiches.

But now it's time for something that got me through the toughest of days, there for me day *and* night. Something that I still love to this day that truly puts a smile on my face.

Now we move to the 'royal level' of foodstuffs. . . .

Cereal.

Yup, breakfast cereal.

They told me it was the most important meal of the day, so I ate lots of the stuff.

You know when you pour cereal into a bowl without checking first to see if you have milk . . . and you don't have milk? Nightmare.

Basically, life is like a big bowl of Rice Krispies. Childhood, teens, school, exams, interviews, jobs, hobbies, relationships, everything is just one great big giant bowl of Rice Krispies.

Imagine an empty bowl and you fill it with Rice Krispies. Just Rice Krispies, no milk yet, please don't get ahead of me here. Just Rice Krispies on their own, nothing else.

How would you describe them?

Plain. Still. Muted. Pale. Crispy. Dull. Dry. Bland. Parched. Basic. Thirsty. Dusty. Boring. Uneventful. Beige. They are simply not exciting. They are lifeless until you add the magic ingredient. . . .

The Milk.

Then what happens?

They come alive. They rise. They Snap, Crackle and Pop . . . they fizz, they bang, they whizz. They float! You can see them moving in the bowl in front of you, some even fall over the side.

Captivating, pleasing, enticing, magical, absorbing, mesmerising, alluring, lively, uplifting.

Basically, you add the milk and shit gets exciting.

But if we don't get stuck in quickly, devour the Rice Krispies, top them up, refresh them and whack some sugar on from time to time, then what happens?

They turn to mush, they become soggy. You don't want them and guess what, neither does anyone else.

So if life is the Rice Krispies then that must make us . . . the milk!

And if we don't get stuck into school, our jobs, our life, then fairly quickly it's going to turn to mush, it's going to become a bit soggy. Life becomes bland.

We need to get stuck in, devour life, top it up when needed, refresh it entirely if we must and whack some sugar on when you have to. Just keep in mind you're not Willy Wonka but still, occasionally, life needs to be sweetened.

Look around, there's an awful lot of mushy and soggy out there.

The world needs YOU.

So, to summarise one last time – this book is a bag of crisps, life is a sandwich but, most importantly, you are the one that can make things happen. The most important relationship you'll ever have is with yourself. Like all relationships, there will be ups and downs but you are the magic ingredient.

Thank you for your time, and to finish this book with three words never been used to finish a book before, the last thing I have to say is this . . .

BE. THE. MILK.

Acknowledgements

Big thanks need to go to Billy Joe Armstrong for the words and the hooks. Vic Reeves and Bob Mortimer for the door you opened in my mind. You guys got me through my teens and changed everything.

And of course, huge thanks to Ali, Kian and Ellis for always supporting this weirdo.

I love you guys. x

About the Author

Gavin Oattes is an award-winning comedian, international keynote speaker and bestselling author. He runs one of the UK's most exciting people development organisations (treeof.com), working with some of the biggest brands in the world to help them be better humans. At the heart of the organisation is the work they do with young people. Gavin and the team have worked directly with over one million teenagers, inspiring and empowering each and every one to be the best version of themselves. He lives in Edinburgh, Scotland, with his wife, two children and his two cats.

Keep Up with Gav

Twitter: @gavinoattes
Facebook: @gavinoattes
Instagram: @gavoattes
Website: gavinoattes.com

Index

exclusion, feeling left
    out 209–10
exercise 236–7
extraordinary, dreaming of
    being 16–17, 79, 84

F
failure
    of comedy journey 68–70
    courage to fail and
        start again 244
    in exams 183–4, 189–90
    fear of putting us off
        our dreams 66
    and goal setting 234
fairness 82, 111
fame
    desire to 'make it' 91–2
    wishing for 64
family
    dying people's most
        important thing 263
    spending time with 163,
        166, 167, 264
    see also parents
fantasy versus real life, Freddie
        Mercury 169
farts 200–204, 230
fear
    of being on stage 10
    and deadlines 182

of failure 66
of flying 227
of leaving home without a
    phone 143–4
fear of the mystery of missing
    out (FOMOMO) 145
fear of joining in (FOJI) 145
Fear of Missing Out
    (FOMO) 144, 246
feelings
    not having the courage to
        express 261
    talking about 203–204, 214
    see also emotions
Finding Dory (movie) 155
    five big takeaways from 155–6
Finding Nemo (movie) 141–3
finish line, mad race to 256–8
fitness, saying yes' to 95
fitting in/conforming
    and not being true to
        yourself 262
    by pretending to be someone
        you aren't 151
    versus standing out 19
    worrying about 84, 255
Flight of the Conchords,
    comedy act 72
FOJI (Fear of Joining in) 145
FOMO (Fear of Missing
    Out) 144, 145, 246

ALSO BY **GAVIN OATTES:**

For when you are older:

LIFE WILL SEE YOU NOW
Gavin Oattes
9780857088086 • £10.99

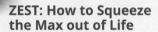

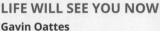

SHINE: Rediscovering Your Energy, Happiness and Purpose
Andy Cope & Gavin Oattes
9780857087652 • £10.99

ZEST: How to Squeeze the Max out of Life
Andy Cope, Gavin Oattes & Will Hussey
9780857088000 • £10.99

For your younger brother or sister:

(For 7-11yr olds)

DIARY OF A BRILLIANT KID: Top Secret Guide to Awesomeness
Andy Cope, Gavin Oattes & Will Hussey
9780857087867 • £10.99

BRILL KID – The Big Number 2!
Andy Cope, Gavin Oattes & Will Hussey
9780857088918 • £10.99

AVAILABLE FROM YOUR FAVOURITE BOOKSHOP OR ONLINE